HIJRAS
THE LABELLED DEVIANTS

HIJRAS
The Labelled Deviants

SATISH KUMAR SHARMA

GYAN

Published by

Gyan Publishing House
5, Ansari Road
Daryaganj, New Delhi-110002
Phone: 011-47034999, 9811692060
E-mail: books@gyanbooks.com

Distribution Network
gyanbooks.com
India, USA, Canada, UK, Australia, France

ISBN: 978-81-212-0266-4 (HB)

Reprint in India, 2024
First Published, 2000

Printed at: Gyan Press, Delhi.

Hijras: The Labelled Deviants
Author: Satish Kumar Sharma

TO

SUMAN AND SUBU

Acknowledgements

The present study "Hijras: The Labelled Deviants" is the outcome of the help rendered to me by my teachers and friends. I, therefore, consider it my great privilege to express my deep sense of gratitude towards all of them. To begin with, it was Prof. Prakash N. Pimpley, my teacher, who suggested to me to work on Eunuchs (Hijras). Since there was hardly any work available on the subject the study seemed to be an uphill task. However, it was Prof. Pimpley's help and inspiration that the study could make steady progress. For all his help I remain indebted to him.

Since the field work constituted the major and most vital aspect of the study, I wish to put on record the help and cooperation of Mr. Vijay Shandilya, my cousin, who helped me by arranging a meeting with a hijra. It is in the context of my first encounter with a hijra that I would like to mention the timely help of Prof. A. Mahajan, currently Chairman of Department of Sociology, Panjab University, Chandigarh. An unhealthy situation arose after the interview with the first case at village Kansal near Chandigarh. The contact-man, through whom the hijra was approached, was assaulted and threatened by the latter of dire consequences. Prof. Mahajan, on my request, immediately responded and with the help of police solved the problem. It was because of that further field work could be carried out. I express my sincere thanks to him.

In carrying out the field work, my friend and class-fellow, Mr. S.S. Shergill, currently advocate, Punjab and Haryana High Court, Chandigarh, helped me enormously. He accompanied me to different places and even interviewed one of the most informative and important cases at Jalandhar. His constant help and encouragement was in fact the pivot of the entire field work. I thank him.

It was with the help of my teachers and friends that the first report, in the form of a dissertation, could be prepared. Subsequently, two papers entitled "Eunuchs: Past and Present" (The Eastern Anthropologist, Vol. 37, and later abstracted in Sociological Abstracts of ISA) and "Hijra: A Study of An Atypical Role (with Prof. P.N. Pimpley) (Avadh Jr. of Soc. Sciences, Vol. II and later abstracted in Sociological Abstracts of ISA) were published. This renewed my interest in the subject. It was at this time that I happened to meet Prof. Serena Nanda of John Jay College of Criminal Justice, New York (USA). My brief discussion and subsequent exchange of articles with her helped me tremendously. In fact, her comments on my already published papers helped me to make necessary amendments in my already written draft of this book. For the cooperation and useful comments, I remain grateful to Prof. Nanda.

I also thank Prof. Rajeshwar Prasad, Director, Institute of Social Sciences, Agra University, Agra; Mr. Thomas Smith, with whom I could correspond through Prof. Prasad; and Prof. A.M. Shah, Department of Sociology, University of Delhi, Delhi; for sending me their respective papers. In fact, their papers were the only literature to begin with in the context of hijras. Also, I would like to make special mention of my friend, Mr. Mohinder P. Singh, for carefully going through the draft of this study and making useful comments for certain necessary modifications in the introductory chapter.

I wish to mention my wife, Suman, who is a constant source of encouragement to me. She inspired me to complete this work. Her careful readings of the work helped in clarifying many ideas expressed in this book.

Last but not the least, I sincerely thank Mr. Pardesi for the excellent typing of the manuscript.

Chandigarh SATISH K. SHARMA

Contents

1

Introduction

Human society is a complex organisation of human role relationships. The implication of such a structural conception is that the human beings act and interact with each other in accordance with the role they play. Their role performance in relation to each other is further conditioned by the status they occupy. The most basic criterion of defining status and a corresponding role for any individual in any society has been sex. Accordingly, men have been assigned certain specific type of roles to perform and women certain other. Sometimes, the society expects both men and women to discharge some roles jointly or interchangeably. Such and many other type of similar situations present a general case of role performance and, therefore, do not become an object of curiosity for people in the society. This way, the individuals continue to act and interact with each other in accordance with the patterned and institutionalized framework of role relationships in the society. While carrying out their individual roles individual actors also act as observers to others' behaviour. In the process they, in their day-to-day life, come across numerous situations in which certain types of roles, actions and behaviour are let to pass as normal. However, though, rare certain situations exhibit a role which may look normal but the performer of that role by behaving in a specific manner, sometimes creates a freak and an unusual sight and becomes an object of curiosity for the onlookers.

Very often on the streets of Indian towns and villages one sometimes comes across an unusual sight of a group of closely shaven persons in female attire, singing and dancing, making overtures to onlookers, cracking sexually charged jokes at men and making loud clapping sounds with their hands. To non-Indians and also to many Indians these individuals may look very interesting and outlandish freaks of nature. Not because they sing and dance but because of their ambivalent physical appearance. They shave, smoke and talk like men but dress and behave in a more feminine way. To the onlooker's mind one question which would immediately strike relates to who are these people, male or female ? And if they are neither males nor females then what ? In the Indian society these people are popularly referred to as 'Hijras', 'Khusras', 'asexuals', 'middle-sexed', 'neutrals', 'eunuchs', etc. All the terms included in the nomenclature used to describe the indentity of these people have one thing in common and perhaps the most decisive one that there is something wrong with their sexual organs.

At this juncture, two questions that would be inevitable to anyone are : Who exactly are hijras ? And how do they differ from the rest of the human beings in the society and therefore, become an obejct of curiosity for the onlookers ? It is very difficult to answer the question that who exactly are the hijras as there is not one but a number of descriptions given by few scholars who have attempted indepth studies on them. One of the beliefs is that they are castrated males and hermaphrodites[1]. Keeping in view the sexual aspect Nanda argues, "He (hijra) is a third gender role in India, who is neither male nor female but contains the element of both. He is an intersexed impotent man, who undergoes emasculation in which all or part of genitals are removed".[2] Similarly other beliefs about them also amount to their description as "normal males, physically hale and hearty, born with normal genitals and testicles (which may or may not be castrated later) and attire in female garbs".[3] In all the three explanations castration of genitals and putting of female garbs appear to be the dominant features which help us to categorise and designate these so-called males in female garbs as hijras.

The above referred to features, however have a number of significant implications. First, when we describe them as normal males putting on female garbs, then their identity comes very close to transvestites. The immediate issue of concern then is, can hijras be called as transvestites ? Probably, such a deduction merely on the basis of their dressing pattern may not be an appropriate thesis. The hijras, in view of the prevailing beliefs about them, do not behave like transvestites. Transvestites are those normal human beings (male or female) who for the gratification of their sexual needs or some other motives best known to them, may put on the dress of the individual of opposite sex and then behave in the manner in which the members of the group they have joined behave. This is basically done to hide their sexual identity from the larger numbers in that group. Such a behaviour amounts to a deliberate act and is oriented towards a particular goal. The individuals involved in the said act may never expose their actual sexual identity to the members of the opposite sex which they imitate for a specific time span. Since the hijras do not fear to expose themselves, therefore, they cannot be described as transvestites. Then what they are ? In view of the existing definitions about them we may assume that their dressing style somewhat resembles the transvestites but their motives do not. They are not transvestites, is further confirmed by the prevailing popular belief that they are castrated males. The transvestites are not castrated males. The common characteristic between a hijra and a transvestite is not their dressing in garbs of the opposite sex but their deviation from the expected way of life. A transvestite deliberately conceals his identity and tries to achieve his motives. On the other hand, a normal male by getting himself castrated violates the legal codes. Though Indian Penal Code remains silent on the question of castration or inflicting injury on oneself yet the very act of undergoing such an operation under section 319 and 320 of the code amount to causing grievous hurt[4]. Whether the injury is inflicted against oneself or against others is certainly a crime especially in view of the legislation brought about by the Gaekwad of Baroda in 1880 which declared castration a crime[5]. Thus, the act of emasculation which hijras are believed to be undergoing is a deviation from the existing legal orders of the state.

Contrary to whatever has been said about who are the hijras, many hijras themselves claim[6], that their sexual deformity is biological in nature and not an injury caused by themselves. It is a controversial issue, especially when referred to the claims of those who have made studies on hijras and the claims of some of the hijras themselves who say that they are true hijras and have not got castrated. Since the present work is concerned with those persons who claim that they suffer from a condition in which there is some deficiency of sexual development[7], it is, therefore, desirable to look into whether their claim is factual or not.

In genetical terms, the birth of a male or famale child or a child with the characteristics of both the sexes is possible. According to the science of genetics the nuclei of human contains a deploid number of chromosomes, consisting of twenty two pairs of autosomes and twenty-four pairs of sex chromosomes, which make a total of forty-six. In the ovum, the sex chromosome is always X, but in the spermatozoa it is either X or Y. The relative number of X and Y carrying spermatozoa is always equal. The fertilization results in forty-six chromosome patterns carrying either an XX or XY combination, i.e., a genetic female or genetic male respectively. But sometimes in very rare cases many male children are born with underdeveloped, hidden and deformed genitals. In such cases it is assumed that the child born is a girl. On the other hand, a girl child may be born with an abnormally developed clitoris and may be assumed that she is a boy. Sometimes, owing to genetical defects, a child may be born with the characteristics of both the sexes. In the science of genetics, persons having characteristics of both the sexes are described as 'Hermaphrodites', a name derived from a Greek God Hermes Greek Hermes, the messenger of God—a mischievous and essentially a masculine character) and the Goddess Aphrodite (a symbol of love)[8]. The hijras do exhibit the characteristic features of hermaphrodites especially the mischievousness.

In the light of the foregoing explanation it becomes somewhat possible to arrive at a probable sociological view-point regarding hijra identity. It seems reasonable to define hijras as males or females who are sexually deformed. Being sexually deformed, they are not capable of reproducing. Inability to reproduce, in view of the cultural traditions of Indian society, is socially disapproved. Any such individual is singled out in the society. It is on account of sexual deformity that the hijras become stigmatized. In any human society there is always every likelihood that people, in general, would practice discrimination against any stigmatized individual. The sense of stigma practised, as Goffman puts it, perhaps, is never less than that of Greeks, who originally coined the term on the basis of visual aids to expose something unusual and bad about the moral status of an individual.[9] In relation to stigmatized persons, it has been maintained,

> "By definition, we believe that a person with stigma is not quite human. On this assumption we exercise varieties of discriminations through which we effectively, though unthinkingly, reduce his life chances. We construct a stigma theory, an ideology to explain his inferiority and count for the danger he (possibly) represents."[10]

What is implied here is that it is not merely the biological state of an individual which makes him different from others but there is also the public response to such a state and attachment of a particular type of identity to his being which earns him a status and corresponding role in the society. Since the hijras are singled out as stigmatized persons and the society recognises them to be socially and biologically incapable of performing the expected roles of the male or female gender they therefore, are not accepted as part of the main stream and, thus, left to lead a life of their own. Maybe it is because of their isolation from rest of the society that by putting on female garbs they tend to pass as normal human beings which is apparently observable from hijras' way of life and manifest behaviour. Not only that they also, as stated in some studies, try to rationalize their existence in the society by citing historical figures who, they believe, were hijras. For example, the hijras of Gujarat associate themselves with Bhima and Arjuna, the two great characters of the epic Mahabharata.[11] Moreover, these individuals through such rationalizations in the society seem to be managing their life and continuity of their role. This type of behaviour is not only found among hijras but is also akin to deviant individuals and groups in human society[12].

In view of the foregoing we hypothetically take hijras either born as hermaphrodites, a deviation caused by mal-development of genitals, or they, contrary to the normative expectations, get themselves castrated and acquire the stigma of asexuality, thus, leading a life identical to that of deviant individuals. The congruence between their and the identity of deviant individuals and groups is further evident from their other attributes. The available scanty literature suggests that they either live in organization of their own, have a specific code of conduct, and enter into anti-normative activities, such as homosexuality[13], in which they act as passive reactors. In the given socio-cultural gestalt of Indian society homosexuality is considered as an abnormal activity which is also contrary to the normative order of the society. With a spoiled identity and engagement in the non-normal activities, like homosexuality, the hijras are, therefore, assumed to be deviants and their activities as deviant behaviour.

How far is it justifiable to conceive hijras as deviant individuals? While this question calls for a detailed study of hijras' life, the use of the concept of deviance itself needs to be qualified before its application to any category of human beings. The reason being that the concepts of 'deviance' and, deviant behaviour' have specific connotation. It is, therefore, of utmost significance to discuss the theoretical basis of the concept.

The concept of deviant behaviour has been looked at, broadly from two different points of view by social scientists and criminologists. Its most frequent and widespread usage has been in terms of 'violation of social norms', signifying departure from the norms laid down for the regulation of individuals' behaviour. The norms conceived as standards of behaviour in a society carry along a moral binding force which is socially endorsed as acceptable and appropriate[14]. Such a conception of deviant behaviour remained quite popular in the early researches and textbooks[15]. No doubt that violation of norms continue to be viewed as non-conforming behaviour, however, in the recent sociological writings on deviant behaviour a question is very often raised that to what extent violation of norms amounts to social deviance? In this respect, it has been held that societies tend to tolerate certain acts to some extent. It is only after the behaviour goes beyond the limits of toleration[16] that society may take serious note of it and term it as undesirable and anti-society. In accordance with such a viewpoint, it is not merely violation of norms that constitutes deviance but it is the degree of violation which matters more. How do we then ascertain the degree of violation? In the context of how to do it, Clinard argues that it depends upon the nature of the social situation or the behaviour in question. According to him, there are situations inimical to the welfare of the members of society, such as, murders kidnapping, sexual abuse of young children and incest. Since these acts go beyond the limits of tolerance, therefore, these acts often receive strong disapprovals from the members of the society and accordingly termed as deviant in nature.[17] Further, in comparison to the said there are certain problems, such as mental disorders of neurotic kind which present lesser degree of danger to other members of the society. The reason being that in such situations it is only these, who have neurotic complaints, suffer and not the others. Due to its individual nature neuroses may be tolerated to an extent in a society[18]. It is, thus, obvious from Clinard's analysis that it is not only the behaviour which violates normative order but the one which goes against the welfare of members of the society is considered deviant in nature.

Besides 'norm violation' explanation, the deviant behaviour has also been conceived as an outcome of social interaction process. It is observed by Becker that deviance is the infraction of rules. The rules, which are made in a society, are applied to people. People in the process of their interaction with each other may break the rules and the rule breakers are, therefore, seen as a threat to the society. The deviant behaviour is 'what members of the society so label and the deviant is the one on whom the label is successfully applied.'[19]

The aforementioned suggests the possibilty of emergence of subcultures within a single society as a result of labelling process. This conception departs from the conventional one which relied heavily upon the thesis of violation of social and legal norms. However, in the later case, violation of social norms may or may not be there but it is the labelling which is the important constituent of deviance. For example, the person labelled by others as a homosexual or thief or any other type of deviant may accept this label for himself because of the influences of suggestion or persuasion, or because of the acceptance and support of others similarly labelled. The label recently acquired may provide the recently labelled persons with new friends and which subsequently leads to rejection of the former by old friends. Following which deviance may be understood as a naming process implying thereby that regardless of the act the behaviour must be explained as deviant by some significant elements of a society. Therefore, it is discernible that it is not form of the behaviour per se that distinguishes deviants from non-deviants. it is rather as Kitsuse holds, "the response of the conventional and the non-conforming members of the society who identify and interpret behaviour as deviant which *sociologically* transforms persons into deviants."[20]

The labelling conception of deviance is widely acclaimed in the sociological writings.[21] One can see labelling model as a reaction against the assumption that there is something inherent in an act which makes it deviant. Rather, the focus is taken away from the act itself and placed on the process whereby an act or actor comes to be labelled as deviant and the effect of such a definition on the individual's self-identity. Under this model one can no longer accept the assumption that certain forms of behaviour are per se deviant, for it is not the behaviour per se which activates the process of societal reaction which differentiates deviant from non-deviant. The deviant is no longer seen as "abnormal" but rather as a victim of a label which imputes moral inferiority and essentializes his character into a single generalized definition[22]. Now the question arises as to under what conditions deviance becomes apparent ? And what are the theoretical perspectives underlying emergence of deviant behaviour ?

The problem of deviant behaviour and deviance, perhaps, is as old as the society. Emile Durkheim, the founding father of functional school of thought in sociology, viewed the problem of crime as something integral to human society and exists as something normal. The rationale of his argument is that the concept of 'collective conscience', which Durkheim considers as central to the integrity of a social system, cannot be acceptable to all the members of a society due to the lack of commitment to it by certain members. As such, it is not only difficult but futile to expect everyone's behaviour as alike[23]. In describing such a behaviour as something normal, Durkheim opined, "society where criminal acts are not committed, the sentiments they offend would have to be found without exception in all individuals' consciousnesses, and they must be found to exist with the same degree as sentiments contrary to them. In case such a condition is fulfilled, the crime does not disappear but changes its form and occurs through other avenues"[24].

It has also been argued that deviance has certain positive functions to perform. Because of this, it has been considered not only inevitable but also a necessary aspect which is 'bound up with the fundamental conditions of all social life and for the evolution of morality and law'[25]. It has been stated,

> "Where crime exists, collective sentiments are sufficiently flexible to take on a new form, and crime sometimes helps to determine the form they will take"[26].

This argument is supplemented by Durkheim with a number of examples of people, like Socrates, who by opposing and violating the prevailing collective sentiments paved the way for future transformations. The punishment which is accorded to the violators acts as a healer to the wounds inflicted by the former on the collective conscience[27]. Thus, both crime and punishment are not only inevitable but also functional. Such a conception further elaborated in a number of works[28] emphasized that it is the society that gives rise to deviance for the fulfilment of many of its functions.

Following the basic proposition of the functional school, Merton evolved a social and cultural theory of deviant behaviour, popularly known as Social Structure and Anomie[29]. In fact, Merton has derived the concept of anomie from Durkheim who applied it in the context of suicide. The basic theme of the said theory emphasizes that the deviant behaviour originates from the culture and social structure of a society. Each society maintains a set of cultural values and the members of the society have complete consensus over these. But this ideal situation often gets disrupted due to certain structural constraints. It is alleged that the members of a society are placed in different class positions in the given social structure. It implies that there are structural inequalities which further te inequalities of social and economic types. Being located in differential positions and guided by the values of achievement and competition, all the members of society tend to strive for the attainment of their goals. The organised set of social relationships in which the members of the society are variously implicated and the norms which guide these relationships, however, do not remain constant. At times, the social and cultural structures, especially amidst the ongoing process of goal achievement, may exert pressure and create a typical type of behaviour which is not in consonance with the social and cultural values. Such a situation, in which the normative aspects are abandoned and normlessness prevails, creates deviance[30].

Merton termed such a state as 'anomie' implying thereby "breakdown in the cultural structure, occurring particularly when there is an acute disjunction between cultural norms and goals and the social structural capacities of members of the group to act in accord with them[31]. It is further added that not all the members of a society under the said pressures are prone to act in a deviant manner. But only those 'placed in a particular position in the social structure and exposed to the stresses are likely to exhibit deviant-behaviour'[32]. Most likely, according to Merton, it is members of the low-socio-economic stratum who are prone to deviance. The reason for their deviation is that such individuals do not have adequate resources and educational qualifications for the achievement of higher goals. In order to achieve the higher goals such individuals abandon the institutional means and adopt non-institutional means[33]. Also the major question often confronted by such individuals or groups, according to Merton is 'what in the most effective available procedure in netting the culturally approved value'[34]. Such means provide more of rewards than the institutionalized mean s.

There arises a question whether the non-institutional means, what Merton has termed as 'most effective available procedure', are available to all those who are forced by the society to be deviants ? Since the means are scarce in the society, all cannot have equal access. In a given social structure and due to structural inequalities the members of the society have differential access to social and economic opportunities. This implies that as access to legitimate means is differential, similarly the access to illegitimate means is not equally distributed among the potential criminals[35]. The reason for building up such an argument lies in 'differential association' which provides opportunities for the acquisition of deviant skills and criminal values. It is emphasized that there are specific 'neighbourhoods in which crime flourishes as a stable, indigenous institution and provide opportunities of learning to the young'.[36] It is, therefore, obvious that the structural inequalities exist not only in terms of access to social and economic opportunities leading to generation of deviance, but also among the deviants in the acquisition of illegitimate means as stated above. It constitutes an important aspect of the criminal role performance. Only those who are able to acquire these values get the recognition of professional thief. Individual who does not have the cleverness of a thief, as Sutherland would put it, "would immediately land into prison...a person can be a professional thief only if he is recognised and received as such by other professional thiefs"[37].

Another question challenges Merton's basic premises of 'common values'. Can such common values be found in a society ? In fact, Merton contradicts his own argument by arguing about the existence of structural inequalities and observance of common values. One does not find it convincing to talk of common values when there are sharp distinctions in terms of inequalities of opportunities, life chances and life styles of people. Even Durkheim who talks of collective conscience leaves sufficient scope for dissent, non-conforming behaviour and possibility of crime. The reason being that whatever kind of act of deviance occurs in a society may also be supported by a large number of people who submit their thinking to such ideologies. This also shows that such deviations have a collective base rather than individual[38] as stressed by Merton.

Merton's criticism did result into the formulation of, as is evident from Cohen, Sutherland, etc., a similar but somewhat distinct theory of deviant behaviour, i.e. subcultural theory. As referred to above, this is based on the proposition that some of the social groups in a society establish distinct norms and values. These may or may not be contrary to the already existing norms. While Cohen ultimately falls in line with Merton, some others, however, disapprove both on many grounds. It is rather argued that deviance results from the subcultural systems which emerge in a society due to cultural practices followed by different groups.[39] For example, it is argued that there exists a lower class subculture having its own norms, values and objectives. Such groups though live within the defined limits of the total society yet these tend to maintain their distinctiveness in numerous ways. It is believed that lower class socio-cultural groups do so in order to minimize their own effects upon themselves of their, what can be termed as dissatisfied life [40]. The behaviour of such groups in actual may not be an anti-normative order of the total society. But it is defined as deviant because of its complete isolation from the culture of rest of the society.

The acceptance of the above exposition also presupposes no interaction between the two cultures, i.e., the subculture (conceived as deviant) and the main cultural traditions of the larger society (the non-deviant culture). This cultural distinctiveness of subcultural groups is in relation to the wider culture of the society. In fact there is constant interaction between the two and the larger society recognises the deviant culture as a distinct one. On the other hand, the deviants partially commit themselves to the normative order as very often they would attempt at putting forward justifications, excuses and rationalisations in defence of their deviant acts in the society[41]. This, in fact, forms part of the "learning of techniques of crime and motives, drives rationalizations and attitudes favourable to the violation of law[42]. The learning of such techniques has been termed as techniques of neutralization[43]. This implies that through such methods the deviants not only wish to undo the done but also disown the responsibility of the deviant activities. The charges are often labelled against parents and the society for deviant acts. These kinds of rationale also cast serious doubts against the theory of deviant subcultures. Also as Matza states, the neutralisation techniques often employ some of the norms of the total society to justify their breaking of other norms[44]. The subcultural groups, therefore, are not Isolated entities in the society. They rather remain in constant interaction with the larger society and rationalize their activities by referring to some of the legal norms.

Following the lead provided by Matze, it is discernible that deviants and deviant activities in a society can be found only when there also exist non-deviants and conforming behaviour. They are related with the others in the society. As a matter of fact, it is this very aspect of existence of a definite type of relationship between deviants and non-deviants which has been given very little attention by scholars. This, however, does not mean that there exists a vacuum. There has been few studies conducted by sociologists which reveal that there always takes place some interaction between deviants and non-deviants. Sometimes, as Matza points out that there may be emergence of subculture groups but these may not be posing any threat to the existing normative order. But, be cause such groups live in isolation so there is some type of hostility towards them. Now the issue arises how will such a group be interpreted ? For a better understanding it is desirable to take into account the interactionist perspective of deviant behaviour. This perspective instead of laying emphasis upon the etiological factors such as deviant motivations, pressures, social forces causing deviance etc. stresses upon the analysis of interaction between those who are defined as deviants and those who define them as deviants. The primary emphasis is put on the definition bestowed on an individual or a group by the definer. For example, when an individual is removed to a mental hospital for treatment then he comes into contact and interacts with the staff of the mental hospital. After having a series of interaction the patient accepts the verdit of the staff about himself. That is, when the patient arrives in a hospital he has a different conception of himself. But, when he interacts with the hospital staff his conception of himself changes due to the imposed conception of his self. When he leaves the hospital he does not have the same conception of his self with which he had once arrived at the institution for treatment. These, the so-called total institutions (e.g., hospitals, treatment home, sanitorium, etc.) put pressures upon the individuals to accept the institutional labels or definitions about themselves. Especially institutionalization of the inside environment influences the individuals to such an extent that he is unable to think that he is able to live outside that environment. This process has been defined as 'mortification of the self'[45]. In brief, it is in the process of interaction that some of the individuals accept others' definition about themselves. This is what the interactionists emphasize.

Lemert, for instance, assumes that the deviance or a deviant in a society is produced by the process of differentiation,[46] which also comes very close to structural viewpoint. However, he departs from the predecessors significantly in dealing with the questions who is socially deviant and how one becomes deviant ? A distinction is drawn between two types of deviant behaviour, namely, the primary and secondary. The former category denotes that behaviour which is produced by psychological processes in specific situations and is rationalized as function of a socially acceptable role[47]. Such deviations can occur on account of numerous factors. On the other hand secondary deviation will occur "when a person begins to employ his deviant behaviour as a means of defence, attack or adjustment to the overt and covert problems created by the consequent societal reaction to him"[48]. Now the important factor in the occurrence of deviance is response of others and its consequence for the deviant himself in terms of his incorporation of others' view in his own identity. In other words, secondary deviation is individual's response to others about his own self.

In Lemert's analysis societal reaction is very vital in the determination of deviance. It is in this process that stigmatization of the deviant actor takes place. The total process has been divided into eight parts beginning with primary deviation. The sequence follows : "(a) primary deviation, (b) social penalties, (c) further primary deviation, (d) stronger penalties and rejections, (e) deviation with hostilities and resentments, (f) crisis with respect to tolerance and formal action by the community, (g) strengthening of the deviant conduct, and (h) ultimate acceptance of deviant social status."[49] In a way, the said sequence involves a chain of reactions between the community and the deviants till the deviance is accepted and efforts being made to adjust to the related deviant role by the deviants.

Becker, who is perhaps one of the most popular exponents of labelling theory, however, goes furher than Lemert. While recognizing the significance of interaction and public reaction to deviance, Becker argues that "social groups create deviance by making the rules whose infraction constitutes deviance, and by applying those rules to particular people and labelling them as outsiders.[50] He further makes deduction from his above statement and argues that "deviance is not a quality of the act the person commits, rather it is a consequence of the application by others of rules and sanctions to an "offender". The deviant is the one to whom that label has successfully been applied"[51]. Becker's argument implies that there is nothing which is deviant as such. Whatever is designated as deviant is the consequence of others' perception and definition.

This situation raises a very pertinent issue that under what circumstances an act is defined as deviant ? According to Becker the circumstances leading to definition of some as deviants include the respone of people which varies with time, the status of the person who commits the deviant act. the way the rules are applied and the interpretation of the act by the audience, i.e. the response of people to that act. At the same time, it is observed by Becker that the "rules created and maintained through an act of labelling are not universally agreed to. Rather such rules often become object of conflict and disagreement ; part of the political process of the society."[52] This means that an act labelled as deviant in accordance with the rules of a particular society may not be constituting deviance in another society having opposite set of rules. This aspect is very crucial, as its major implication implies that deviance is culture specific and culturally relative. Each society has its own rational way of treating a particular social phenomenon and social behaviour of human beings.

The foregoing discussion on various perspectives underlying deviant behaviour brings out certain characteristic features. First, deviance is that action of human beings which goes beyond the limits of toleration and consequently perceived as contrary to the normative order by a considerable number of key persons in a society. Further, such an action is responded to by members of the society through public recognition. The 'public recognition' is very crucial in determining deviance and categorization of someone as deviant. Second, the categorization is not without certain socio-cultural basis. There needs to be some rationale, either provided by the members of the society who categorize some as deviants or by the so-called deviant group in defence of its activities and behaviour. Only under such conditions the labelling can be successful. Third, there is a constant interaction between the deviants and non-deviants. Fourth, the deviance is the creationnot only of physiological, psychological, ecological and social interaction factors but also of the society. It is believed that society creates deviance because the latter is functional for the integrity of the society. Related with this is the belief that each social structure has unequal distribution of opportunities. Those who are endowed with these opportunities exhibit a conforming behaviour and those who do not have the required opportunities adopt illegitimate means. Thus, to the exponent of structural viewpoint deviant behaviour occurs in a society due to structural factors. Fifth, deviance is culture specific. Finally, the deviants are rejected by the members of the society and, therefore, treated as some type of outsiders. Now, having said about various characteristics, let us take the case of hijras who also represent some kind of a subcultural group, live in isolation, seem to have their own norms, rejected by the society. But at the same time one finds that there exists some scope of social interaction between them and the society. How do we explain such a contradictory response of the society on the one hand and that of the hijras on the other ?

Hijras, a group of individuals, presenting themselves as third gender role not only remains an object of curiosity to the onlookers but also raise many sociologically relevant questions and provide insights into certain areas, such as deviant behaviour, role development and identity formation, leading to institutionalization of a non-normal role in a society. Assuming that hijra is a full-fledged deviant personality and a role performer the ongoing study would be concentrating on various questions : (i) how a non-normal role is institutionalized; how can there be continuity in such a group based on biological characteristic which paradoxically are negativating reproduction ? Specifically the interest lies in finding out how recruitment and socialization takes place ; what are the generalised rewards which motivate individuals to play this role ? What are the stresses and strains involved in this role ?

In terms of their deviant context, the primary interest lies in studying their social organisation, status in the society, and their relationships within their own group and with the society at large.

'Hijras : The Labelled Deviants' is a study having two-fold objective. First, it seeks to analyse the role of hijras from the point of view of sociology of deviant behaviour. Second, it being entirely a new field of investigation, with very little information available, the study also attempts at exploring and eliciting the social life of hijras in the Indian society. To do so, the author develops his analysis on the basis of whatever literary evidence available and detailed case histories of 19 hijras.

The use of case history method is based on the rationale that this method is useful in studying individual case, group life, a community and an institution. The characteristic feature of this method is that any case studied is assumed as representative of the group and similar cases studied make generalizations possible to certain extent. The social scientists have been using this method fairly in an exhaustive manner in studying professional criminals and other deviants. Another feature of this method is that with this method alone the researcher is able to make use of various social research techniques, such as interview, observation, etc. and various documents equipped with a bearing on the subject concerned and all such materials which may enable a social scientist to have a vast knowledge about the problem.

In accordance with the objectives, the study proceeds with the analysis of hijras in terms of their status and role, both in the past and present day Indian society. This chapter is based upon the available literary sources. The subsequent chapters are based entirely upon the cases interviewed by the author. Each chapter includes detailed excerpts from case histories and analyses are, therefore, carried out in the light of the information imparted by the respondents.

NOTES AND REFERENCES

1. Dr. G.R. Salunke, "Cult of the Hijras", *The Illustrated Weekly of India,* August 8,1976, p. 14.
2. Serena Nanda, "The Hijras of India: Cultural and Individual Dimensions of an Institutionalized Third Gender Role", *Homosexuality,* Vol. II(3-4), p. 35.
3. A.P. Sinha, "Procreation Among the Eunuchs", *Tne Eastern Anthropologist,* Vol. 21, No. 2,1967.
4. Salunke, *op. cit.* 1, p. 21.
5. *Ibid.*
6. According to a news item published in *The Tribune* of 13th October 1986, Mr. Bhola, the President of All India Hijra Kalyan Sabha made a mention that though 98 per cent hijras are castrated

yet there are 2 per cent who are true hermaphrodites. He does make mention that there are very rare cases of true hermaphrodites.

7. According to my discussion with a Gynaecologist at Post Graduate Institute of Medical Education and Research, Chandigarh and my enquiries from some of the leading hospitals of northern India, I did not find any case of a hermaphrodite child born during the past one decade. However, I did see the genitals of a few cases among them a male had a short flaccid penis. The testicles were not visible. Tho female hijras had a urinary canal but no vagina. It is, however, difficult to say whether this was the result of castration which they might have undergone some years before. However, the hijras invariably said that they were true hijras except for one case who admitted that he had been castrated.

8. Based on the discussion with a Gynaecologist.

9. Erving Goffman, *Stigma*, Harmondsworth, Penguine Books Ltd-, 1964, p. 11.

10. *Ibid.*

11. Howard S. Becker, *Outsiders*, London, Collier Macmillan Ltd., 1963, pp. 38-39.

12. A.M. Shah, "A Note on the Hijras of Gujarat", *American Anthropologist*, Vol. 36, No, 6,1961.

13. Nanda, *op. cit.*,2.

14. R.K. Merton, "Social Problems and Sociological Theory", in R.K. Merton and R.A. Nisbet *(eds.)*, *Contemporary Social Problems*, New York, Harcourt, Bruce and World, 1961, pp. 697-737.

15. See for example, A.K. Cohen, *Deviance and Control*, Englewood Cliff, N J., Prentice Hall, 1966; Simion Dinitz, *et. al.*, *Deviance*, New York, Oxford University Press, 1969; W.A. Rushing, *Deviant Behaviour and Social Process*, Chicago, Rand Mc Nally, 1969; etc.

16. M.B. Clinard, *Sociology of Deviant Behaviour*, New York, Rinehart and Winston, 1961, pp. 12-14

17. *Ibid.*, pp. 14 20.

18. *Ibid.*

19. Becker, *loc. cit.*, p. 9.

20. John I. Kitsuse, "Societal Relations to Deviant Behaviour-Problems of Theory and Method", *Social Problems*, Vol. 9 (Spring), 1962, pp. 247-56.

21. See for example, Harold Garfinkel, "Conditions of Successful Degradation Ceremonies", *American Journal of Sociology*, No. 61, March 1956, pp. 420-424.

22. K.T. Erikson, "Notes on the Sociology of Deviance", *Social Problems*, Vol. 9 (Spring), 1962, p.308.

23. cf. Emile Durkheim, *The Rules of Sociological Method*, New York, The Free Press, 1938.

24. Emile Durkheim, "The Normal and the Pathological", in Delos H. Kelly's *Deviant Behaviour*; *Readings in the Sociology of Deviance*, New York, St. Martin's Press, 1979, p. 51.

25. *Ibid.*, P. 54.

26. *Ibid.*

27. E.H. Sutherland, *White Collar Crime*, New York, Holt, Rinehart and Winston, 1960.

28. See for details, A.K. Cohen, *Delinquent Boys*, Glenco, The Free Press, 1955; Robert A. Dentler and Kai, T. Erikson. "The Functions of Deviance in Groups", in Delos H. Kelly's, *Deviant Behaviour, loc. cit.*, 24.

39. R.K. Merton, *Social Theory and Social Structure*, Glenco, The Free Press, 1957.

30. *Ibid.*

31. *Ibid.*, p. 162.

31. *Ibid*', p. 162.

33. *Ibid.*, p. 183.

34. *Ibid.*, pp. 134-135.

35. Richard A. Cloward and Lloyd E. Ohlin, "Differential Opportunity and Delinquent Sub-cultures", in Delos H. Kelly's, *Deviant Behaviour, op. cit.*, 24, pp. 122-133.

36. *Ibid.*, p. 124.

37. E.H. Sutherland (*ed.*), *The Professional Thief*, Chicago, University of Chicago Press, 1937, p. 211, cited from Cloward and Ohlin's, "Differential Opportunity and Delinquent Sub-cultures", loc. cit., 35, p. 123.

38. Also see, A.K. Cohen, loc. cit., 28.

39. Walter B. Miller, "Lower Class Culture as a Generating Milieu of Gang Delinquency", in M.E. Wolfgang, *et. al.*, (*eds.*), *The Socio-*

logy of Crime and Delinquency, New York, John Wiley and Sons, 1962.

40. *Ibid.*

41. cf D. Matza, *Delinquency and Drift*, New York, John Wiley and Sons, 1964.

42. E.H. Sutherland, *Principles of Criminology*, Philadelphia, Lippincott, 1955, pp. 77-80.

43. G.M. Sykes and D. Matza, "Techniques of Neutralization: A Theory of Delinquency", in Delos H. Kelly's, *Deviant Behaviour, op. cit.*,24, pp. 100-109.

44. *Ibid.*

45. For details, see E. Goffman, *Asylums*, Harmondsworth, Penguin Books Ltd.,1968.

46. E.M. Lemert, *Human Deviance, Social Problems and Social Contrcl*, Englewood Cliffs, Prentice Hall, 1972; also by same author, "Role Enactment, Self and Identity in the Systematic Cheque Forger", and "Primary and Secondary Deviance", in Delos H. Kelly's, *Deviant Behaviour*, loc. cit.,24, pp, 629-648 and p. 166. To support his view, Lemert quotes Shaw's study emphasizing that deviance develops in purticular areas in which the delinquent children do not have access to cultural heritage of larger society. For details, see C. Shaw, *The Natural History of a Delinquent Career*, Chicago, University of Chicago Press,1941.

47. *Ibid.*, p. 168.

48. *Ibid*,, p. 169.

49. *Ibid.*, p. 170.

50. Becker, loc. cit., 11, p. 9.

51. *Ibid.*, pp. 9-18.

52. *Ibid.*, p. 18.

2

Hijras : Status and Role

The discussion pertaining to deviant behaviour and deviant individuals in the introductory chapter revealed that deviant individuals and groups justify their existence by invoking historical justifications. In defence of their behaviour they build up all sorts of social and psychological rationales. They very often equate themselves with historically well known persons. Can all this be true of hijras ? If not all the above referred to attributes are visible in the behaviour of hijras, however, one thing has been found to be existing among them that they equate themselves with historical personalities. How far the claims of hijras hold grounds ? At this juncture the interest also lies in ascertaining whether such claims made by hijras are to hide their real indentity ? Or had they actually been occupying a status of repute in the society ? With the above questions in view the present chapter makes analysis of the status and role of hijras in the Indian society.

Probably, to a common man, hijras are sexually deformed, physically ambivalent and stigmatized individuals having characteristics of both male and female. These are the features which, in general. help people to identify and designate them as hijras. No doubt, that an analysis of their physical appearances, especially of facial and upper bodily parts, by and large, by anyone, would reveal them as dark complexioned, huge ugly looking and some of them as slim more like females, and very rarely some of them having touch of grace and beauty. This is generally so and common man's description holds true in an empirical setting.[1] Going by the visible characteristics people, in general, conceive them as outcastes coming from poor families. This does not seem to be the case as far as the empirical reality is concerned. The hijras do come from various castes and classes, rich and poor families of rural and urban India, and represent a mixture of all types.[2]

Following the availability the said evidences about hijras, socio-economic profile, this part of the study attempts at analysing the status and role of the hijras alongwith the other questions raised above.

2.1 Hijras : Through the Ages*

Although the claims of hijras can be justified in the light of the existing documentary or textual evidence yet it is also interesting to know that they have been present in the Indian society since Vedic times. Besides that their traces have also been found in the writings dealing with the ancient history of Homeric Greece, Europe, Syria, and during African slave-trading era etc.[3] Most of these writings revolve around the practice of castration carried with various purposes on males and females. This practice in the context of Indian society can be stated to have orignated from the tradition of desexualization of animals. During Vedic period horses were often castrated. Following that tradition it used to

---

*For this portion, I acknowledge the three major sources : Luis H. Gary, *Eunuch*, in *Encyclopaedia of Religion and Ethics*; Thomas Smith *Eunuchs : Ancient and Modern* : and R.N. Saletore, *Sex Life Under Indian Rulers.* I have largely depended upon these sources for developing the present chapter.

be males rather than females who were castrated.[4] Why castration was practised ? The practice of castration was very popular because of a variety of reasons, especially outside India. At the same time it reflected on the status hijras occupied.

First reason for castration was the desire to develop a particular physical and mental make up. It was noted that performance of castration on childern was meant to prevent the development of secondary sex characteristics. Such men could be later on, used as senior slaves to guard harems. Being castrated these men were less attracted towards their families and proved more faithful to their owners and masters.[5] From the realms of historical writings the practice of castration can also be traced back from the history of Babylon where the boys were castrated with the sole purpose of making them eunuchs. The tradition accorded by Ammianus Marcellinus, brings to the fore that Eunuchism as an institution was instituted in Mesopotamian region as its first home.[6] This, as an atrocity, tells Zenophon, was introduced by the elder Cyrus into Persia, where hijras became an institution. Herodotus narrates how Xerxes sent certain boys, some of whom happened to be illegitimate children, under the guardianship of Hermotimus, his chief eunuch. Hermotimus, in turn, took them to Sardis where he sold them at higher prices. This was the second purpose served by castration.

The practice of castration further spread to Persia and other eastern countries where it held an interesting place in the life of that society. The hijra, as a man, was nothing still he rose to very high position of trust. Nevertheless, he retained his efficiency and powers of vengeance which he could carry out with a surprising sense of completion. Under the king Darius, hijras occupied high positions in the Persian courts.[7] The source of their availability was castration, a practice through which the kings obtained and presented them as gifts to each other. A classic case of similar nature comes from Babylon and Assyria countries which were obliged to send to king Darius, as a tribute, 500 castrated boys. History further apprises that the Ethiopians every year sent to the king of Persia, Cyrus and also Cambysus, besides numerous gifts, a band of five such boys. The practice continued till the days of Herodotus during 5th century B.C.[8] Its third purpose was exchange of gifts and obligations by the kings to each other.

Hijras, according to the traditional accounts maintained by Ammianus Marcellinus, were early known in Assyria where they apparently acted as 'governors and generals'. They were also in Israel at least as early as the reign of Jehu. In Greece, the practice of castration prevailed by the time of Persian wars.[9] "Origens, a Greek writer, as much celebrated for the easiness of his manner, humility and modesty, for his learning and sublimity of his genius, was surnamed Adamautus from his assiduity and became so rigid a Christian that he made himself a hijra (eunuch) by following the literal sense of the text in the Greek Testament which speaks of the voluntary eunuchs of Christ"[10].

The practice of castration in ancient Greece also existed as a form of punishment. It was also practised in the shrine of Syrian Goddess, Gallos, on certain days. The available literary evidence suggests that the multitudes assembled at the shrine, practised self-emasculation and offered oblations. The young ones castrated themselves by leaping into the middle of the assembly with a sword and then running through the city they flung into a house the part they castrated. In return, they received from it the feminine dresses. Lucian, discloses that Gambabus, an intimate friend of Syrian King, Autiochus Soter (280-261 B.C.) castrated himself in order to save himself from the ignominy of committing adultery with Soter's wife. Mention is made of castration of women in Lydia by Xanthus. He apprises that the Lydian king, Adramyttes "was the first who had women castrated in order to use them instead of male eunuchs (hijras)"[11].

The most interesting instance relates to Roman empire. It is believed, "in the degenerate days of the Roman empire, eunuchs were regularly made soon after reaching puberty, for the sensual gratification of Roman dames. From remote antiquity, the orientals, as also at a later period in Greece, hijras were employed to take charge of women, generally as chamberlains. Their highly accessible pasition in harems of princess enabled them to have influence over their royal masters to a considerable extent. Through which they could also raise themselves to the stature of great trust and power".[12] In view of the different type of status and role of hijras it is discernible that their recognition in any country depended upon their usefulness. Where they were not useful in those situations they were made hijras to suffer. For instance, in Egypt castration was imposed as punishment for committing adultery.[13] Even in China during the 8th century B.C., the laws of Alfred the Great, punished a servant through emasculation for raping a female servant. All male relatives of a Chinaman condemned for treason were doomed to death, excepting the young who were castrated for service in the imperial palace. Castration was also performed in certain countries where oriental influences were present.[14] Also one can trace the incidences of sterilization of criminals and people suffering from certain diseases. The latest advocate of this practice was Hitler of Germany[15].

The vivid picture of hijras reveals one unique characteristic feature. Accordingly, it can be stated that in European and Eastern lands, the hijras were purposely made. The reasons, as cited in the preceding brief account, were embodied in the highly selfish motives of kings, slave traders and men of high esteem. Rarely, one could come across self-mutilation. But such instances also bring in view the cruel laws of various countries. In a way, such a heinous practice could be nothing more than the abuse of power. Even where the hijras were elevated to the positions of governors and generals that too was for the protection of power and wealth and winning over of loyal subjects. By and large, hijras were socially and legally condemned and were doomed to live a life of social, sexual and other kind of material deprivations in Europe and Eastern countries.

In the Indian society too the hijras enjoyed a fate mixed with ups and downs from time to time. But unlike other countries, the history suggests presence of born hijras. In fact, hijras in India claim themselves as belonging to a third gender,[16] and to justify their claim they very often tell a story from Hindu epic Ramayana :

> "In the time of Ramayana, Ram had to leave Ayodhya (his native city) and go into the forest for 14 years. As he was going, the whole city followed him because they loved him so. As Ram came to the edge of the forest, he turned to the people and said, "Ladies and gents, please wipe your tears and go away". But those men who were neither men nor women did not know what to do. So they stayed there because Ram did not ask them to go. They remained their 14 years and snake hills grew around them. When Ram returned from Lanka, he found many snake hills. Not knowing why they were there, he removed them and found so many people with long beards and long nails, all meditating. And so they were blessed by Ram. And that is why they say that they are respected so much in Ayodhya"[17].

Some observations made on the basis of collection of historical instances evince that in the western part of the Bellary district of Madras and in the adjoining portions of Dharwar and Mysore, men who are born eunuchs or in some way deformed wear female dresses and are mistaken for women[18]. This is an evidence which supports the definition of hijra elicited in the previous chapter on the one hand and further draws distinction between the hijras of India and outside India, on the other. However, the author does not rule out the possibility of castrated hijras in the past and contemporary Indian society. A question worth exploring here is what has been the role of hijras in the Indian society in the past? This might throw some light on their role as deviants.

In Vedic India, the acclaimed ancient and best form of Hindu society, the hijras do not seem to have enjoyed any status. They were considered as men of low caste and carried on dancing role. A citation below depicts people's attitude towards their role :

> 'When I was in my mother's womb, eunuchs danced at the door; so I am lame and have no hair on my head'.[19]

Furthermore 'in a human sacrifice of the Vedic period, hijra was the victim offered to Misfortune (Papman) and—in this case the victim being neither of Brahman nor of Sudra caste to Prajapati'.[20]

During The Mahabharata (an epic with whose name also goes a particular time period) hijras were again described as persons of low status and who could not be permitted to be around king while he was having consultations.[21] The possible reason again for no such permission to them was their lowest social position. It has been argued,

> "Mlechchhas (barbarian, non-Aryans) are the dirt of humanity; oil-men are the dirt of Mlechchhas; eunuchs are the dirt of oilmen; and they who appoint Ksbatriyas as priests in their sacrifices are the dirt of eunuchs"[22].

While many such evidences make one believe that hijras occupied a low status, certain claims contradicting the above versions do come up for some considerations. Especially, when one finds a widespread belief among the hijras of Gujarat who associate themselves with Bhishma and Arjuna, two well known characters of Mahabharata. They believe these two characters were hijras[23].

Though there is no direct evidence to refute the tall claims of the hijras, yet certain historical recordings of different epochs do tell us of their high status. During ancient and the medieval periods of Indian history they were existing as an institution. In the fourth century B.C., they were employed in the harems. This role of their, in fact, was very significant in maintaining the personal hygiene of the harem inmates and in the administration of affairs of the harems. By performing such role they worked for the king's happiness. But in spite of the benefits which the rulers derived from the hijras in the palace and harem, the latter, however, were denied certain fundamental rights[24].

The employment of hijras in Hindu courts is believed to be quite common during the 2nd and 5th century A.D. The king selected hijras for the sentinels of his antahpura. Even during the medieval times, hijras were considered as the notable features of the court life. In the Vijayanagara harems each of the queens had a house to herself. It is strongly held that no man was allowed to enter these premises but for hijras who enjoyed access to queens' quarters. They could visit the queens any time they liked. Whenever the queens desired to go out loitering they were essentially accompanied by a guard of three to four hundred hijras to protect them. Their primary role was to see that all other people kept a long distance from the queens. Being great favourites of kings and recipient of high salary they were even employed inside the royal kitchen. Excepting them and women none could stay inside the kitchen. For instance, the emperor Achyuta Raya's kitchen had ten cooks who prepared food. There was one hijra posted there to guard the gate of the kitchen. He never allowed anyone to enter the kitchen precincts for fear of poison. The king was served food at table only by women and hijras.

During the Muslim period they held positions of esteem. Though in general, every mutilation of beasts and men was forbidden by the Prophet Muhammad and He, expressely, enjoined upon his followers not to make themselves or others hijras, yet those who underwent such an operation, were highly appreciated and their value was always much greater than that of non-castrated slaves. Also Muslims employed them either as guardians in the harems of princess, in the house of men of high ranks and great wealth, and in the sanctuaries. Burckhardt writes, "Many of the lower classes in Mecca kissed the hands of the hijras of the great Mosque on approaching them. Their chief was a great personage entitled to sit in the presence of the Pasha and the Sharif".[26] They were sent as presents especially to the great mosques of Mecca and Medina[27].

In the Muslim courts they were recognised as persons of importance and they occupied high statuses. Muhit-ul-Mulk, a hijra was employed as the Kotwal during the kingdom of Sultan Muzaffar Shah II of Gujarat. Not only that they also held political importance. During the reign of Alaud-din-Khilji, it is believed that hijras began to interfere in court politics and acquired political importance of an unusual type. They became the instruments of several court intrigues and even participated in battles and conquests. The star hijra, Malik Kafur, occupied a unique place during the Khilji reign. Malik Kafur gained political power over the king to such an extent that he, according to historians, dismissed Khizr Khan, the rightful heir.[28]

During the Mughal period, particularly, during the reign of Shah Jahan, hijras held very high positions. They were also employed during the rule of Akbar. It is observed that some of Akbar's nobles developed a veritable mania for these persons. One of them, known as Khwaja Saras Hilai, who joined Jahangir's service, built a town, Hilallabad. Another hijra, Ikitiyar Khan was his *Vakil* and another Itihar was the *faujdar* of his *jagir*. In the royal household of the Mughals there was not one but several principal hijras.[29] According to Smith, "Akbar the Great, got a mosque built in Lohamandi, Agra, at the request of a saintly hijra, Yatim Shah, whose own and his three disciples' remains are buried in its vaults below. An Urs is held at the mosque in honour of Yatim Shah annually, a week after Muslim festival of Shabe-barat"[30]. Similarly, on Gwalior road, opposite the present military farm at Agra, there exists another monument—the tomb of Firoze Khan known as Gommut. Firoze Khan was a hijra at the court of Akbar the Great and was the founder of Firozabad town.[31] Itwari Khan is another notable hijra from the court of Jahangir who became so important and influential that a red stone monument known as Itwari Khan's tomb, originally the tomb of Sikander Lodhi, was later utilized for his burial.[32] In the institution of Khawaja sarais hijras controlled the affairs. Originally Khawajasarais were themselves hijras who were employed in the harems and exercised great influence. The word Khawaja Sara became a title for administrative officers of the harem. The eunuch was a full-fledged man as any other civil or military man. He could be transferred to any other department, civil or military[33]. The same kind of institution was adopted by Rajputs because of their coming too close to the Mughals[34].

A brief but interesting historical account of hijras in the Indian society, to the author, is very revealing. It may be argued that in general human beings tend to reject everything which falls outside the generally accepted. Even the natural phenomena are discarded due to their unusualness. Hijras, who are the victims of genetical defects are not accepted as human beings. When the society looked down upon such beings then why some were made so by the kings by way of castration ? The answer to this question comes from the fact that men of power for their selfish ends encourage and carry on such practices by making certain heinous rules.

On the other hand, the asexuality of hijras proved very useful for the kings. Being no threat to the chastity of kings' women they became an essential part of the life for kings. Their biological incapacity to perform sex won them the position of incharge of women. During the early Hindu court life, later in the Muslim courts and Mughal reign, they also got the position of trust. The possible reason for rising to position of governors and generals was property. As they did not have their families to look after, they could carry on their role in a more dedicated manner and with honesty. As they would not go in for property building, hence they became favourites of kings. Because of this reason the kings never hesitated to get the castrations done either by way of punishment or otherwise.

The foregoing simply raises a question who were deviants—whether those who ordered castrations or those who got castrated under the rules of the governors of the society ?

2.2 Hijras in contemporary India

There may be several questions with regard to the existence of hijras in the minds of many, such as: Are they outcastes? Do they come from condemned homes? Are they not cared for by their parents? What type of existence do they have in the society? These questions are of primary interest as these also reflect upon the question who exactly are hijras?

To begin with the general background, it may be noted that all the cases represent different socio-cultural background. All of them come from different states in India, such as Punjab, Orissa, Uttar Pradesh, Himachal Pradesh, Tamil Nadu and West Punjab (now in Pakistan). Besides their respective states of origin, which give a fairly good account of the widespread hijra cult in India, these people differ from each other in more than one way. The most important dimension creating further differentiation is place of residence. This raises a sociologically relevant question, i.e., what significance this feature holds when the hijras have already abandoned their homes and parents?

The significance of place of residence, hypothetically saying, lies in author's contention and general prevailing proposition that urban and rural residences have differential determining influences on the life of an individual. The difference between the two communities (rural and urban), besides being based on the nature of economy, is also visible from the nature of the existing social structure and consequently patterned set of interpersonal relationships. With little scepticism, it may be assumed that rural and urban residence have a direct bearing on the length of hijras stay, with their parents. Accordingly, the information indicates that hijras with rural background had a shorter stay with their parents in comparison to hijras born in urban areas.The reason being that the identity of an individual is difficult to conceal in a rural setting. The ecological structure of village society is such that it provides a milieu of physical proximity with each other and has certain places of common gatherings where all sorts of information about the village is disseminated and discussed. On the contrary, impersonal life style of the urban dwellers very often hampers the changes of physical proximity and the dissemination of certain type of information. The analysis with regard to place of residence reveals that the hijras having rural background have shorter stay with their parents than the hijras from urban areas. Especially cases numbered as 1, 3, 4, 5, 6, 9, 12 and 16. In these cases, their asexuality could not remain a secret in their respective villages. The stigma of asexuality compelled many of these hijras and their parents to depart from each other. The stay of some of them was even limited to a few days.

In the said context, it is interesting to know how case 6 had to leave his home and parents at the age of twenty days. Not only that, in view of the contention, this case also provides sufficient insights with regard to the difficulties one has to face in a village setting in concealing sexual identity on the one hand and how, after the disclosure of sexual identity, difficult it is to bear the burden of stigma. The head of a hijra Dera, who apprised the researcher, said,

> "When Kamal (the name of the Hijra) was just twenty days old, the village mid-wife disclosed that Kamal was neither a male nor a female. He was a hijra. This news spread throughout the village like a wild fire. Kamal's mother, fearing the consequences, took him away to Jalandhar to her relative's place. But back-home in the village, Kamal's sexual deformity had become a talk of all and sundry. All the members of Kamal's family, who were till date accepted as normal human beings, became stigmatized. The next day brought further ills to the family. A relative came to village and informed that Kamal's mother, due to shock and fear of losing his son, died soon after reaching relative's place. The child was also brought back with the dead body of the mother. The death did not move the people. They informed the hijra who used to visit the village about Kamal. The hijra,

accompanied by his colleagues, came and took away the child".

On the contrary, those born in urban areas could escape the stigma and their subsequent departure for a considerably long time. Hence, some of them could receive the love and affection of their parents. Even they could go to school for some education and lead a normal life in the family environment. The case number 2 and 15 represent classic history of their long stay with their parents. Case 2 explains:

"I was the third child born in a family of five. I had two elder brothers who, in spite of my deformed sexual state, loved me very much. I was put into school and received education upto middle standard. Thereafter, I joined my father in his shop. I always wore boys' dress and was treated as a boy only. I did not mix up with school children much. It was told to me by my brothers and parents that I should not put off my clothes before anyone in the school. Though in the beginning I did not know why I was asked to take such precautions. However, when I grew in age, I could see difference between me and others, especially whenever I came across a boy or girl urinating. This difference often made me think why I do not have the sex organs like others. Whenever I tried to ask anyone I was simply reminded of big dangers. When I grew up, I often used to wonder, "Mein aadmion ke tranh rehta hoon per meri janana chall logon ko shaq mein daal deti thi. Ab log mujhe hijra bhi keh ke pukarte the" (I used to live like men but my gait was feminine. That could put people always into doubts about my identity and they used to call me hijra). At this time I was about fifteen years old and secondary gender characteristics also started appearing. Also at that time, due to some incident for which the stigma of my asexuality was responsible, led me to abandon my home".

The foregoing narration suggests that the identity of an individual in the urban areas can be concealed for a longer duration in comparison to rural areas. The narration made by case 15 makes this more obvious. The case in view is of a female hijra and represents one of therare types. Beautiful looking, young and educated upto matriculation comes from a middle class Khatri family of Uttar Pradesh. She was the only child of her parents. She explained,

> "I was the only child of my parents. I was put into a school at the age of 4 and completed my primary education from an English medium school. I was brought up as a girl. The secrecy of my sexual identity was kept in such a way that even our neighbours never suspected my asexuality. Always clad in female attire, I behaved in a perfect feminine way. My parents were so cautious of my sexual identity that after I completed primary school, they took me off from the school. Rest of my education was only at home. Why was I taken off from the school remained a mystery till I myself became conscious of my own physical condition. Once in my childhood, I remember, on seeing a hijra, I enquired from my mother who he was? But my mother had only tears in her eyes. She simply told me that this is a curse of God. But strange developments in my body, i.e., masculine and feminine, both at the same time, also bothered me. I would insist on taking medical treatment for the ambiguities in my being but my parents simply cried. People living in the neighbourhood started calling me hijra. I could hardly move out of the home. Even if I went out it was only at night. The life became impossible. If I could stay for a longer time at home it was only because I was totally isolated from the social sphere. How long could I live within the four walls of the house?"

While indicating the possibility of escaping stigma in an urban set up the contents of the narration also make it explicit that all this could be possible because of complete social isolation of case 15. Had it been some rural area, the possibility of escaping stigma would have been minimum as the rural areas provide no opportunity of social isolation.

At this juncture it is worth arguing that the place of residence is just one variable and this too is not the sole determinant. It is also important to take note of economic background of their respective families. The reason being that the family resources not only influence life chances but also have effects on life styles, such as place of residence etc. The data recorded in the context of economic aspect evince that the widely held view that hijras belong to condemned category of families is not only wrong but also does not have a pedestal to dwell on. Though there is no case coming from a very rich family yet on the basis of some (cases 2, 11 and 15) it can be said that they do come from economically comfortable families. For example, the father of case 2 had karyana shop. The respondent's family was doing well and maintained good standard of living. The elder brother of the respondent, who was employed in some factory, could afford to leave his factory job to join other members working in family's karyana shop. In the light of the information it can be stated that the economic activity of the family had the capacity to absorb other family members. It was also because of good economic condition that the respondent could receive education upto middle standard. His not going in for high school and dropping out from the school was due to the stigma which had come to be established by that time, and not due to economic constraints which very often is the case with the school drop-outs.

Similarly, case 11, a fair complexioned male hijra, comes from a Rajput family. The family of origin of the respondent owned some land with orchards and other immovable property. The respondent had six brothers and three sisters elder to him. Due to the fear of his sexual deformity being exposed he was not sent to school. The family made informal arrangement of his education at home. Since the family consisted of a large number of children, the case in view did not face any problem as far as keeping of children's company was concerned. He passed his early fourteen years of life with the family and enjoyed all the comforts which a child in economically better off family could have.

From the age of seven onward, he started going for work on the family lands and orchards with his family members. When the respondent was child he could not differentiate on the basis of sex or sexual organs. He was given a male name. Since he was dressed like a boy his identity could be easily concealed from others. However, when he grew ten years old, he started feeling unusual developments within himself. By the age of fourteen, he saw his breasts developing like females. This was not only strange to him but also made him realise that there was something pathologically wrong. Non-development of sexual organs, which is not generally the case in normal populations, made him somewhat doubtful about his perfect male identity. He had heard of hijras. He, by comparing his state, started equating himself with hijras. Whenever he used to go out the people living in the neighbourhood called him Khusra, a term used to designate a hijra. This was the beginning of the end of his association with his parents.

Now, what is more important to note in this case is that the parents being relatively economically well off could protect the child from others' eyes and manage stigma. So much so that they used to pay some money every month to a local hijra, as per the discolsures made by the case himself, in order to keep the child with the family. Besides that family's large size also protected the child. The reason being that since the case could have company of his brothers and sisters at home only, he never felt the need to mix with children outside the home. This way the biographical conditions, especially the economic and demographic, had been instrumental in prolonging case 11's stay with his parents. Even case 15, about whose urban residence, some description was given earlier remained with her family due to relatively good economic conditions. On the basis of the descriptive accounts of family's economic background, it can be argued that relatively better economic conditions proved an asset to the respondents.

Besides the above mentioned cases, there are few others, who come from families with relatively satisfactory economic condition. This is the case of those who represent neither rich nor poor class. They were simply able to sustain themselves and their children without any difficulty. Their occupations were either shop keeping or service in some government office (for instance, cases 4,8,9,10,12,14, and 19 come from such a family background). Like the hijras from good economic family background most of the cases from satisfactory living economic background also had somewhat good early life spent with their parents. For instance, case 4, a female hijra with fair complexioned and beautiful looks was born in Punjab in a small town. Her family, Bania by caste, had a small business in that town. Being first and the only child in the family, she was brought up as girl with great affection and care. At the age of 5 years, she was put into the school where she participated actively in sports and cultural activities. She acquired proficiency in dancing and singing as any other talented child would do. At that age she never knew anything about her spoiled identity. She, being one of the intelligent students in the school and cultural activities, was always treated like a girl. Consequently her mannerism, actions and behaviour were always feminine. But an abrupt end come to her joys as she grew older and ultimately left her home at the age of 12 years.

The story of case 4, however, does not reflect upon other cases as their experiences had not been uniform. Case 8 is one such case among the hijras coming from economically satisfactory family who had very different experiences of life in comparison to case 4. The case under consideration is an introvert one with many reservations. A fair complexioned, wrinkle faced, female hijra, she comes from a lower middle class family of a Tamil Nadu Brahman. The sexual abnormality and conservative traditions made her parents to send her away to her maternal grand-parents who were living in a town at some distance. She was put into the school where she received primary education. But it was not all that easy going. As per her rememberances she used to find herself isolated from her peer groups. Not only that she was also always addressed as hijra. All this often made her inquisitive about the term. Her enquiries often revealed no answer. With the feeling of dejection and gloom she began saying,

> "All those years spent in social isolation made me rigid and blunt against anything and everything. The concept of relationships died for me. One day, fed up with my living, I thought of ending my life. But I could not succeed. However, I did not feel like staying at my maternal grand-parents' home. One day, when I was about ten years of age, I left the home quietly for the unknown. My first place of arrival was Madras. I thought of meeting my parents there. But my mind raised a question that why should I go to my parents who never gave me any love and affection? I was quite new to that place and had no acquaintance with anybody else. There I begged, wandered in the streets for the whole day and slept on footpaths at nights. All those days and nights I often faced many miscreants of young and even old age who on finding me sleeping alone would come and lay by my side. Due to such happenings each night I changed my place. This way the life continued till I matured."

While narrating, she laughed, paused for a moment and then continued,

> "One night, a police constable questioned and took me to police station. I was under his custody. Since I was quite good looking the constable took me for a normal girl. At night when there was no activity around, the constable approached me for having sexual intercourse. But his approach was not direct. He first tried to induce me by offering tea, food etc. Then he started embracing me. I

was scared, not of rape or any sexual activity, as it was not possible, but of disclosure of my actual identity. Such actions of the constable also made me think as to why I was brought to police station for no fault of mine. In the meanwhile, he asked me to come to a dark room adjoining duty room. The moment he found that I was neither male nor female, he, in anger, slapped me on the face and kicked my buttocks. Then he let me go."

After narrating this incident she clapped the way hijras do and made mockery of men who usually fall for females. Anyhow, that was one experience but she had some good time too. She further started saying,

"As luck would have it, the next day, I came across a man, who got me recruited in a private dramatic company-virtually a nautanki. I was trained and assigned the role of a nautanki clown. I worked there for five years. In five years' association, a young man working in that nautanki got interested in me. When he expressed his willingness to marry me, I got scared. I told him of my sexual deformity and exposed my body to him. The quality of physical structure which had started emerging by that time, could not hide my identity. The same night I left that place without informing anyone. I decided then to lead a different life. But again the fear of stigma drove me from one place to another. Unsettled socially and economically insecure, I wandered from one place to another. My early childhood made me hard hearted."

On the contrary to above referred to cases, the remaining eight (1,3,5,6,7,13,16 and 18) come from poor homes of labourers and those carrying out unclean occupations, such as that of sweeper and some about whom nothing is known. In general, the children from poor homes have a very difficult and hard childhood. But in the case of hijras, besides the drudgery of their poverty, they had another most dangerous thing to manage, i.e., their stigma of asexuality. Almost all of them have been the residents of rural areas where their spoiled identity created many problems. Because of which many of them had a very short stay with their parents as noticed earlier. However, their poor economic conditions and the nature of occupations followed by their parents added considerably to their problems. Among the cases referred to above, leaving aside case 7, who is a castrated man, rest were having almost similar childhood with no love and affection of parents.

It is, however, desirable to pinpoint a case having altogether different experience. This is case 3, who comes from a Bania family of Uttar Pradesh, quite old, sick and ugly looking male hijra. Ever since his birth, he has been living with hijras. What he could recall at the time of interview about his childdood in his own words was,

> "Chahe main munda see ya hijra, main ohi haan jo mere Guru nein dasya. Chahe main is halat wich jamandru he see par main ik gal yakin naal keh sakda haan ke jadon to mainu hosh aya hai main apne aap nu hijrian wich he dekhya hai"*.

Whether these lines were only meaning his childhood or a satire on the society, as a whole, is difficult to single out here. But what was important to note was that due to his poor family background and no financial support to him by his parents in the early childhood, he had to suffer the indignities and make his living by the sweat of his brow. He informed,

> "I was told that I was initially living at Bareilly. At the age of two I was sold to a hijra for Rs. 200/—. I used to work as a servant for the master. In fact, everybody in the hijra home was senior to me and, therefore, dictated terms. Sometimes I used to fetch them cigarettes from a nearby shop and at other times, I brought other household requirements. If I refused or showed any reluctance to

---

*Whether I was a boy or hijra, I am what has been told by my master. Whether I have been in this condition since birth, but one thing which I can say with certainty is that ever since I attained consciousness I have seen myself among hijras.

carry out the assigned job, I received beatings. It was often told to me that they had paid to get me. In a way, I was a slave. I grew gradually as a female baby. Alongwith my physical growth, my assignments also changed. I started cooking food for the elder hijras and washing their clothes. Till the age of thirteen I lived with them. But then a secret deal was struck by the head of the home with another hijra. Thereafter, I came down to Punjab with my new master. I was young, healthy and quite mischievous. After coming to Punjab, my master prepared me for the professional life".

The childhood of case 3, while indicating what kind of problems he faced, also points out the possible slave trading which goes on among hijras. This is not only this case which has pointed out this practice but there are two other cases (5 and 13) who did make a mention of this practice. The analysis of their biographical conditions suggests that hijras coming from low socio-economic status background have to face more problems and undergo rigorous working as victims of slave trading.

The data on background profile further throw light by unveiling the fact that hijras are not the men of low castes, as has been maintained in the historical writings and also as a view which may be held by many in the Indian society. They represent almost all the known castes, namely Bania, Brahmin, Khatri, Rajput, goldsmith, Sheikh and some of the castes of scheduled castes. The reason being that when it is the question of hijra by birth, it can happen wlth any caste. At this juncture it may be made obvious that the births of such cases are, however, very rare as per my enquiries from certain leading hospitals revealed. This is what makes many scholars believe that all the hijras are castrated. There is, of course, nothing to deny the fact that some people do become hijras because of castration. Even case 7 is a castrated scheduled caste hijra. However, it is not right to accept that all the hijras are castrated. Anyhow, the point which needs to be emphasized here is that in terms of caste they come from different castes and do not represent any particular single caste. This castewise account, however, gives rise to a very particular question, does caste background affect the childhood of hijras in any way ? Probably, not much can be said about this as final. The reason being that some of the higher caste hijras had very painful childhood experiences than the scheduled castes. For example, case 3, a Bania by caste, worked virtually as a slave during his childhood time and so did case 13, a member of the scheduled caste. What is common between the two is their poor eeonomic background and not their castes. In the light of this what emerges important is the structural inequalities which, in fact, play a very important role. This argument does draw considerable support from those cases who come from economically better off families and as such whose childhood had been somewhat better. Also such cases could acquire some education, stay with their parents for longer period and the like.

To sum up, the analyses of background profile and childhood indicate certain specific features which not only help in unveiling the unknown but also suggest some sociologically important aspects of human beings and society. Firstly, the hijras, like other individuals in the society, have heterogeneous social and economic background. Sociologically, they represent structural variations with regard to their background which have tremendous role to play in determining the quality of their life in childhood. Secondly, the stigma of asexuality does not pardon anyone of them. Here, the structural variation helps varyingly in the defence and management of stigma. Most of the cases who could live with their parents for larger number of years, ultimately became victim of their stigma and had to leave their parents. In a way stigma of asexuality as such and the strong sense and consciousness of stigma in the public are very crucial aspects in the context of Indian society. If such individuals are condemned and considered as outcastes, probably, it is the stigma which makes them so. Otherwise all of them say,

"We are the progeny of the union between normal male and female".

NOTES AND REFERENCES

1. The physical description of the 19 cases contacted was as under :

	Male Hijra	*Female Hijra*	*Total*
Dark complexioned	7	3	10
Fair complexioned	3	6	9
Total	10	9	19

2. The following data speak of hijras' background profile :

   (i) Castewise : Brahman—1, Khatri—7, Bania—3, Rajput—1, Goldsmith—1, Scheduled Castes—4, Sheikh—1, Does not know—1.
   Total—19.

   (ii) Family background : Labourer/Poor family—7
   Small business shopkeeper family—4
   Priest—1, Middle order employee—3
   Rich/Landlord/Orchard Owner —4
   Total—19.

3. For details, see, Luis H. Gray, "Eunuch", in the James Hestings (ed.), *Encyclopaedia of Religion and Ethics*, Vol. V. New York, Charles Scribner's Sons, 1908. p. 579.
4. *Righveda*, I, xxxii, x. cii, 12, cf. Gray, *Ibid.*
5. Luis H. Gray, *op. cit.*, 3, p. 580.
6. R.N. Saletore, *Sex Life Under Indian Rulers*, Delhi, Hind Pocket Books (P) Ltd., 1974, p. 192.
7. *Ibid.*
8. *Ibid*, pp. 192-93.
9. Luis, H. Gray, *op. cit.*, 3, p. 580.
10. *Ibid.*, p. 582.
11. R.N. Saletore, *op. cit.*, 6, pp. 194-95.
12. Luis H. Gray, *op. cit.*, 3, p. 583.
13. *Ibid.*, p. 582.

14. *Ibid.*
15. Thomas Smith, "Eunuchs : Modern and Ancient", *History and Political Science Journal*, 1958.
16. *Satapatha Brahmana*, v.i., 2, 14, iv, lf, cf. Gray, *op. cit.*, 3, p. 583.
17. Sarena Nanda, "The Hijras of India : Cultural and Individual Dimensions of an Institutionalized Third Gender Role", *J. Homosexuality*, Vol. 11 (3-4), 1985, p. 37.
18. See, Luis H. Gray, *op. cit.*, p. 581.
19. "Temple, Legends of the Punjab", in Gray, *op. cit.*, 3, p. 583.
20. Vajasaneya Samh. xxx, 5, 22, in Gray, *op. cit.*, 3, p. 583.
21. *Mahabharata*, XII, xxxiii, 55, in Gray, *op. cit.*, 3, p. 583.
22. *Mahabharata*, VIII, XIV, 25, in Gray, *op. cit.*, p. 583.
23. A.M. Shah, "A Note on Hijras of Gujarat", *American Anthropologist*, Vol. 63, No. 6, 1961, p. 1328.
24. R.N. Saletore, *op. cit.*, 6, p. 192.
25. *Ibid.*, pp. 196-198.
26. *Ibid.*
27. *Ibid.*
28. *Ibid*,, pp. 200-202.
29. *Ibid.*, p. 203.
30. Thomas Smith, *op. cit.*, 15.
31. *Ibid.*
32. *Ibid.*
33. Dr. R. Nath, "Some Important Aspects of Mughal Architecture with Special Reference to Monuments of Agra", in Thomas Smith, *Ibid.*
34. *Ibid.*

3

Institutionalization of a Non-Normal Role

In the previous chapter it was noticed that the stigma of asexuality and emerging crisis of gender identity drove some of the cases studied away from their parents, kinship circles and homes. The most problematic consequence of their spoiled sexual identity is not only their rejection by the society but also many other problems in the overall development of their personality, social behaviour and social adjustment. The current analyses are, therefore, oriented towards an understanding of the total process of stigma management and overcoming of identity crisis. The primary question of concern is institutionalization of a non-normal role.

The process of institutionalization, which in general concerns with the internalization of norms and values of a given social group or society and mechanism of social control, involves a continuous process of socialization. It begins right after the birth of an individual in society. The individual, who is, first of all, a product of a given biological stock, "passes on its qualities to the individual through the genes by an interchange of characters that gives each individual a biological structure and a set of tendencies and dispositions."[1] Such a conception of an individual not only reduces him to a mere biological organism but also divorces individual from society. The reason being that the pathological make-up of an individual is considered to be having a pervasive impact in the determination of his personality. Indeed, one may agree that biologically inherited properties are significant in enabling individuals to learn. The learning, however, is within the given boundaries of the society and not in isolation from others. Furthermore, the existence of individual in society not only implies his age, sex, class, occupation and other attributes but also his relationships with others. It is what produces at the first instance a 'social being' and secondly an environment conducive to the production of a social being through the process of learning.

The characterization of individual as social, therefore, implies the reflection of his traditions, institutions, values and solidarities[2]. It is this aspect of individual in the society which not only helps in the making of the individual as social but also the society as a cluster of acting and interacting social beings. The two aspects of individual and society described above seem to be in a paradoxical situation, i.e., the individual producing society and society producing individual[3]. In Cooley's words, "society and individuals do not denote separable phenomenon, but are simply collective and distributive aspects of the same thing, the relation between them being like that between other expressions, one of which denotes a group as a whole and other the members of the group"[4]. Since both, the individual and the society, are responsible for shaping each other, both evolve and adopt mechanisms through which the process of moulding of individual and society begins. This process is widely acknowledged as the process of socialization which takes place, by and large, within the given normative and value structure of the society.

It is indeed the process of socialization which humanizes

the biological organism and adds the most significant characteristic to it, i.e. social. Since social signifies culture, traditions and an identity, therefore, the process of socialization is very vital as it is through this that culture is transmitted and the individual in the capacity of a thinking and acting unit gets fitted into an organized way of social life. This implies that when individual adopts some of the values of the group life through the process of transmission of culture he modifies himself in accordance with the adopted values. Moreover, when he designates an individual as an acting and thinking unit of the group or society it means that the individual has acquired through his experiences some degree of creativity and rationality. In the words of Mead, this is the stage of creation of self in an individual which contains his own thinking and the thinking of others, vis-a-vis certain social phenomena.[5]

Apart from cultural transmission and creation of self, the process of socialization helps individual to learn socially approved habits and form certain types of attitudes; learn certain skills through the practice of which individual performs specialized roles in relation to others in the society. The concept of socialization, therefore, implies a process of learning, by and large, within the given framework of norms and values of a society.

The foregoing argument raises two vital issues. One, how the socialization is facilitated in the society ? The primary concern here is with the agencies which prove useful in the process of socialization and have a lasting influence upon the individual. Two, what modes are followed by socializing agencies ? With regard to the first, it may be argued that primarily two types of settings, i.e., formal and informal, facilitate socialization of the individuals. The formal settings refer to schools or vocational institutions and the informal refer to family and peer groups. Primarily the role of informal settings have tremendous influences on the development of individual personality and his abilities to perform the social roles. The research studies have shown beyond doubts the impact of the family, family's class status and other correlates have a positive correlation with learning abilities and performance of role.[6] This is because of the fact that different families provide differential opportunity structure for exposure and access to various persons and objects. According to Mead, in the early stages of one's life the social interaction is limited to few, who are specific individuals surrounding the child. The behaviour of child is to a greater extent determined by his experiences with those surrounding him and who are not merely others but "significant others."[7] It is, therefore, suggested that individual's interaction with others and his experiences resulting out of the process of his interaction help him internalize others' attitude towards himself and, thus, learn appropriate behaviour which is expected from him by others. The process, therefore, goes on throughout one's life.

There is no doubt that most of the learning about various things in life depends upon the opportunity structure, exposure to various things and social interaction based on experiences with others. The total process, however, does not guarantee conforming behaviour. The possibilities of deviation cannot be ruled out. It may be recalled that while discussing on deviance it was said that values and norms are cultural specific and certainly lack universal application in many cases. Since socialization itself is culture specific, i.e., carried out in view of the dominant values of a group or society, therefore, certain degree of non-conformity is always found in societies.[8] In fact, such a situation even arises during the process of socialization itself.

This brings us to another issue that in case there is projection of non-conforming behaviour then what should be done? This question is related with the issue concerning mode of the socialization raised above. The psychologists, especially, those dealing with child development and the process of socialization state that there are two ways of socialization.[9]

The first refers to 'repressive socialization' which takes place in a situation of asymmetrical relationships guided by the dichotomy of authority and subordination. In this process 'obedience' is the most cherished value. In the case of violation of this value the emphasis is laid down on punishing the violator. On the other hand, the second method is described as 'participatory' socialization under which involvement of the child is the underlying principle. In this situation the child is granted autonomy in thinking and acting so that creativity develops in him. The motivation comes through the rewards which are presented either materially or symbolically to the child for learning and projecting good behaviour.[10] In the larger context of group or a society what shall be the way, will in all probability depend upon the nature of group and its goals. The reason being that since socialization aims at transmitting culture and preparing the individual for the attainment of various goals through enacting certain kind of behaviour and performing the expected roles, therefore, the method of socialization will be adopted accordingly. Following which, it may be argued that individual socialization and his subsequent learning and taking of role, whether a conscious or an unconscious act, will depend upon the way he is socialized. As a matter of fact, the total process, right from the creation a of a self, identity formation and role taking, makes individuals adapt themselves to the culture and traditions of the group or society.

Following the foregoing discussion the author assumes that the role of hijra is also an outcome of the process of socialization, especially in the context of its institutionalization. Before getting on to socialization and other related issues first, an attempt is made to deal with the issue of identity crisis and how the hijras overcome this in the society.

3.1 Identity crisis and Problems of Adjustment

Having known the fact that hijras, being sexually deformed, carry a stigma, the said biological condition of their causes identity crisis for them. According to hijras themselves this state of their makes their acceptance very difficult in the society. The fear of stigma is so strong among general populace that it not only drives hijras out of their homes but also put into danger their families' relationships within the kinship circles and also hinder formation of new relationships with others. For instance, case 2 narrated how his presence in the house affected the formation of her family's relationships with other families through matrimonial alliances. She said.

"As I told I had two elder brothers. When I was about sixteen years old, our family started with the idea of marrying my elder brother who was about twenty two years old at that time. The matrimonial alliance almost materialised with a family which was very close to our family. Since the family knew about me already and somehow disclosed this to some of family's close ones, enormous pressure started mounting upon girl's parents. They started yielding to whatever fears were expressed by their relatives. Finally the relationship which was near establishment broke off unceremoniously and cast a gloom all over. In fact, when girl's father came to say all that I was at home. I could hear the refusal occurring due to my presence, It was not the end. This also started estranging my relationships with other family members. But they tried to hide from me, may be they did not want that the uncordiality of our relations become talk of public. Anyhow, two-three more such happenings took place. These instilled in me bitterness about my own self. I started thinking what is the use of my staying with the family when the family members cannot feel happy and comfortable. In a way a silent conflict was on within my own self and with rest of the members of family. One day I left home with some money which I had saved for myself. I straightway went to Sri Lanka and wrote a letter to my brothers; (some of the lines in the letter which she spoke to the author in Hindi were, "Ab mein aapke pas kabhi bhi nahin aoungi. Mere se tumhara badnami hai, nuksaan hai, isi liye tumhe munh nahin dikhaungi. Aap shaadi karo, ghar basao, hamesha khush raho"). "Now I will never come to you. Because of my presence you people have to bear insults and loss. I will not show even my face. You get married, make family and live happily. So, that is how, I tried to resolve the ongoing conflict within me and with others in the family. But the conflict with the society began when it ended with the family."

The foregoing narration is a sufficient evidence to the fact that the sense of stigma and its fear is so strong that it ultimately creates a situation of crisis and drives hijras to go out in search of some other place to which they can call their own. In other words, they move out in search of their own self, an identity which can instill in them a feeling of we, a feeling of belonging to some group or society which can explain their consciousness about their existence.

The above cited narration of case 2 should not be assumed as a specific, isolated incidence and lacking application to hijras in general. There are, in fact, many other such cases having similar experience. For example, case 4 also faced similar identity crisis from the age of 12 years onward. The moment she became conscious that she belonged neither to male gender nor to female, one question "what is my gender" troubled her the most. She tried to seek answer to the said question from her mother. It was told to her that she was a hijra. It made her sad. She had also learnt that if the hijras came to know that a hijra was staying in a family, they took her away at any cost. On the other hand, she had many occasions to watch the hijras in the streets and at people's houses. Their life, which she could visualize on the basis of her observations, often made her think of the same life for herself in the coming future. What is important here, is that individual's own perception of an anticipated situation. In this context, the fear of stigma being attached to oneself and the family of origin conditions individual's action to make exit from the nears and dears. That is what exactly happened in the case of case 4. Similarly, case 14 is in no way different from case 4. In her case also it was due to the fear of stigma by her family that she was compelled to leave the parental home.

One important question which follows the above description is that how after leaving their immediate family environment, such individuals are able to manage the identity crisis and the burden of stigma. The obvious answer to this question, with reference to those who joined hijra cult, can be that such individuals get recruited to hijra group. But it is not always the case. Many other cases show that they make abortive attempts to manage identity crisis by going from one place to another. Their life histories demonstrate this to a greater and convincing extent. Accounts of wide travels and transitional period in hijras' life produced below indicate how they attempt to manage identity crisis and stigma.

The case 2, after leaving her home at Madras, went to Sri Lanka. But in few days' time she was deported back to Madras as Sri Lankan authorities objected to her illegal entry. After staying at Madras for few days, she went to Bombay, a long journey from south to west. There, she worked as a porter at the railway station. During all that time she disguised herself as a boy. This was easy as she had thick growth of beard and she would not shave for the fear of being caught as a hijra. She did not have porter number and the licence. Because of which many a time she would be beaten up by the policeman on duty. This was done as policemen often suspected her a pickpocket, which she was actually not. Whatever she could maange to earn she would use that for her food, cigarettes and sometimes for a quarter of hooch. She used to sleep on footpath where some hijras, as per her narration, used to run a kind of prostitution centre (hijras practising sodomy and acting as passive reactors to men for a meagre sum of Rs. 2/- a man). One day, as she was drunk, she entered into a dialogue with the hijras living there. Somehow, under the influence of liquor she abused them for their doings. The agitated hijras, in order to teach this disguised man a lesson, tore off his pyjama. This act of theirs' disclosed her real gender. For the whole next day she remained with them. But at night she ran away from there and got into a moving train.

She left Bombay for ever and reached Nagpur. There, she worked in a hotel as dish-washer for a couple of days. Eventually, she also learnt cooking. This gave her a new indentity. She got employed in a house as a cook. She worked there sincerely for qutie some time. However, one day on being spotted by an old acquaintance of her, she left Nagpur also. She arrived at Secunderabad and started working as the porter. Being working at a railway station she made herself very mobile. She could not stop at Secunderabad for a long time. From there she travelled to many places, namely, Assam, Calcutta, Kashmir and Amarnath. The fantastic thing about her early travels is that she travelled without ticket. But now she does not even dare to take a chance as she has money to spend. It was a long period of five years during which she acted as a male and which also helped her to hide her real identity. From Kashmir, she came down to Punjab, first at Ropar and then finally to Chandigarh. A question, why she wore male dress during all these years was raised to her. The answer to the above question, vis-a-vis, her sexual position was appropriate to certain extent. The remarks stated,

> "Izzat ke liye aadmi ka kapda pehanti thi. Larki ka kapda is liye nahin pehnati thi ki kahin koi such mein larki samajh ke chher na de. Jawan thi main. Chahe main khusra thi prantu sunder thi. Jawani mein to kute ka bachcha bhi sunder hota hai chahe uski koi bhi nasal ho. Main to mard ki beti thi".*

* For respect, I dressed myself in man's clothes. I purposely avoided putting on female garb. I feared that anyone may mistake me for a female. I was young and good looking too. In young age even dog's pup is beautiful and I was the offspring of man.

The foregoing description highlights a very important feature of male dominated societies in which anything other than manliness is considered weaker and, thus, made prone to any kind of exploitation. This is more so when one is passing life as an individual and does not have any affiliation with any human group. In such a situation, passing as male is something thought of as symbol of social security. Such kind of defence mechanisms are often employed by hijras to make some adjustment with the society before their permanent affiliation with any hijra home or group.

The foregoing description pertaining to search for identity raises a very pertinent question, i.e., what is the end of disguised and unsettled living? Can the adoption of various kinds of defence mechanisms to hide the spoiled identity help the hijras pass their total life? To what extent the hijras are successful in concealing their actual identity. And similarly, many other questions can come up. Besides the appropriateness of these questions in the given context, these were also specifically discussed with the respondents during the course of personal interviews with them, which has been sociologically quite revealing.

First, it was revealed by the hijras (only those who joined hijra homes in their later ages) that their wandering from one place to another provided them sufficient experience and time to think about their future. Second, sometimes it is in this process that they got struck up with a particular way of life and, thus, tend to pass their whole life just like that. But at this juncture they also state that successfully leading the life of a male is not always possible. In this context the description of some of the cases given in the foregoing speaks similarly. The concealed identity gets disclosed at some time or the other. This is quite natural phenomenon when one lives and interacts with other human beings. Third, there is always a tendency among them to identify themselves with what actually are. This tendency, however, is not something natural alone but socially conditioned. This conditioning occurs in the process of hijras' encounters with the members of the society at large, in their rejections even by their own families under social pressures etc. As a matter of sociological fact it is the social pressure asserted on them either through stigma theory or by projecting an individual socially inferior that the hijras are forced to look out for something of their own. A detailed description of some of the cases will indicate how the whole process works and pressurises them.

Case 11, finding himself in a fix, started going to watch hijras whenever he got an opportunity. The question, how he started identifying himself with hijras, was put to him. He replied,

> "When I was sure that I did not have a place either in male or female worlds then I started identifying myself with hijras. But I did not know anything about how they live where they live and what sort of life they lead. In order to get an answer to the questions rising in my mind I thought it worth to go and watch hijras. Initially, whenever I saw any hijra, I tried to get close to him, by watching, talking, sharing cigarettes, bidis, etc. with him. After meeting them I used to come back and stay aloof for hours together. During this period I would sometimes act, talk and behave like a hijra. I do not know what all that was. But it certainly provided me some relief".

This is the first stage when one, with spoiled sexual identity and being fed up and dejected with the behaviour of others in the society, starts identifying himself with the hijras. Interestingly, another case when asked what was that which made him to identify himself with hijras, provided sociologically very significant information. According to him a very important factor is others' behaviour towards persons like me. When the society constantly keeps on inflicting a scar of one's spoiled idetnity then one is made to think that his place is not in the home where he is born. It is somewhere outside it. The effect of such a feeling is that one develops an inferiority complex. With such a state of personality development one just gets ousted from his kith and kin circles. That is what happened with many who joined the group of hijras voluntarily. The second important factor is who can accept a hijra. In this context one always feels that only those who are of the similar identity can prove closer and accept a person with a similarly spoiled identity. That way mentally one begins to tilt towards them. Third factor which is a natural phenomenon that one has an instinctual push. According to one of the hijras, "there is a famous saying that (a line from a Punjabi folk song) Nachchan vale di Addi na Rehandi (i.e., a dancer cannot help taking dance steps). One who has to dance for others, cannot live away from dancers."

The three factors are sociologically very significant, especially, in the context of sub-cultural group formation. The similarity of character helps in the formation of social relationships. That too in a situation in which the emotional security is very badly needed and sought. This aspect in most of the cases becomes a decisive factor to dissuade them to abandon their bid to pass as a normal male or female.

However, on the other hand, though someone is able to manage himself to pass as a male or female for a considerable time period, yet certain unavoidable circumstances force them to identify themselves with the hijras. For instance, case 14, a female hijra was able to go to school in a female guise. But her accident and hospitalization proved too much. The so far concealed identity could no longer be held concealed. Finally, she had to come with hijras for the rest of her life. Similarly, other natural factors, such as physical development, growth of hair on the face and chest, non-development of breasts, choked voice etc. are the ones which make their concealed identity more obvious thus forcing them to look for a similar identity and at last ending up with their bid to conceal themselves by identifying themselves with their counterparts living in separate homes, away from the society at large.

This way the three questions pertaining to their wanderings in disguised fashion come to an end with the emergence of a feeling that their final resort is hijra home. This feeling, in the light of the foregoing account, occurs not only naturally but to a greater extent conditioned by social factors. It is also desirable to mention here that the search for identity and the understanding of one's own self is the first step towards institutionalization of a non-normal role.

3.2 Self-Identification and Recruitment

The last and the previous to last sections noted that irrespective of their class and caste background the hijras were neither in a position to adjust themselves in their families of origin under various socio-cultural compulsions nor in the society due to their rejection on account of their ambivalent physical make up. The consequence of which was that some of them (for example, case Nos. 1, 3, 5, 6, 9, 12, 13 and 16) could have a stay only for a period ranging from a few days to the maximum of three years with their families as the local hijras took them away from their parents. On the other hand, the remaining cases (2, 4, 7, 8, 10, 11, 14, 15, 17, 18 and 19) who had from a minimum of 6 years to a maximum of eighteen years' stay. However, one most significant development which could be seen as emerging out of the identity crisis was that they were forced by the circumstances to look for a new home. The development of self and its identification with the hijras ultimately made them decide to affiliate themselves with hijras. The acquisition of membership of a hijra home and learning to behave as hijras are the two vital aspects from the point of view of institutionalization of a non-normal role. It indeed becomes sociologically very significant, especially when the group to which the hijras seek membership has more of a diffused socio-cultural as all the members of such a group come from diverse socio-economic, regional and linguistic background. Moreover the recruitment sought is not always granted simply but it involves formal procedure which is accorded socio-historical justification by the hijras. In view of the title of this section, the ensuing analysis will concentrate on how the cases studied have been recruited to hijra home, i.e., the pattern of recruitment. Second, with reference to institutionalization what motivations do the hijras have for joining hijra home on the one hand and what motivates the hijras of hijra homes to recruit new hijras on the other. These questions will, thus, provide answer to the earlier query, that is, how does a group, which is biologically negativing reproduction, continues to exist.

There may arise many question regarding how the recruitment takes place among hijras. But all such questions will be best answered by the description of the way hijras get recruited. In general, there are two dominant patterns of recruitment. One voluntary and another coercive. The former deals with two situations in which the hijras are either handed over to professional hijras by the parents themselves or when the hijras grow young, they themselves opt to join the band of hijras. The second pattern, however, concerns with a situation in which the coercive approach is adopted. This type of practice is conditioned by resistance put forth by the parents or the individual himself and the alleged customary right which permits hijras to take away any person who is a hijra. Of the total cases studied, 13 belonged to voluntary category and 6 to coercive category. At this juncture, I shal however, reproduce some excerpts from the case histories to provide a true picture of how recruitment is done (i.e.,) by both voluntary and coercive means).

To begin with the case of voluntary recruitment, it is worth mentioning here that in this category there are six cases (Nos. 5, 6, 9, 12, 13 and 16) who were handed over to hijras by their parents. But all these were given away at different ages. Case 5, 6 and 9 were barely 5, 20 and 10 days old, respectively. As a matter of fact, they themselves do not know under what conditions they got recruited. However, they have got little to say on the basis of whatever they could learn from their elders in the homes they are currently living in. Cases 5 and 6 narrated that they were handed over to hijras on a condition that their parents would be allowed to come and visit them in the Deras ; whereas cases 9, 12 and 13 were given unconditionally.

This conditional and unconditional recruitment of hijras has two sociological implications. First, the conditional aspect indicates some degree of relationship between the hijras and his family of origin. It is a very natural phenomenon. The enquiries made revealed that up to a considerable length of time period such children continue to receive love and affection of their parents through the mutual visits. Subsequently, with the increase in age of these children the frequency of meetings between the hijra child and parents decline. Another reason for decline is the physical mobility of younger hijras from one place to another. On the other hand, unconditional parting of the parents from their children is, many a time, governed by the fear of stigma, evidence to which has already been cited in the previous to last section.

Besides the above, sometimes the economic condition of the family not only becomes decisive but also gives rise to a very unfortunate social situation in which the parents sell the child. It happened in respect of case 6 who comes from Uttar Pradesh. The author's meeting with the head of the Dera evinced a very significant fact which speaks, on the one hand, of poverty of his parents, and on the other hand poverty of the society in which such events occur and pass unnoticed. The Guru said, "This chella of mine belongs to a very poor familly. When she was initially acquired from her parents by the head of a Dera in Uttar Pradesh that head paid Rs. 300/- to the parents on two considerations. One was that the parents were very poor. Two the parents demanded money as compensation. From that day onward till the age of ten years she stayed in Uttar Pradesh. The beautiful hijras have a good market. At a meeting of the hijras I met her and her ex-Guru. I talked about her coming with me. The Guru told that she had purchased her for Rs. 300/- as a child. Since she had given her training and also made her professionally competent, she would not sell her for less than Rs. 3,000/-. I bought her by paying her the said amount thinking that she would give better returns".

The foregoing except from the interview, while indicating how poverty compels even the parents to part with their child and earn out of it, also brings into notice the practice of trading among hijras. At this moment, it is however, difficult to say to what extent such practice of trading prevails among the hijras in contemporary times. Nevertheless, this type of freak case does point out one fact that in the recruitment process sometimes money also performs a very important function.

Apart from the above kind of voluntary recruitment there is another kind in which the hijras get recruited at a later age. As has also been seen earlier in such cases, though the parents endeavour to hide the spoiled identity of their wards for quite some time yet they remain unsuccessful in resolving the inner conflict in their wards caused by spoiled identity. Therefore, the wards move out and wander from place to place. They however, find their final resort in the hijra homes. Among the cases studied there are six such cases (Nos. 2, 4, 8, 11, 18 and 19). It is important to know as to how do they get into Deras. Knowing about the method of recruitment to the Dera is also important because it involves the motivational aspect for the new member as well as for those who are already the members of hijra home.

The case histories of all such cases reveal that in the society at large the non-acceptance and continuous run from one place to another make hijras' life miserable. The miseries, desire for a stable life and melancholic state of mind make them realise that they cannot live in isolation from the hijras living in Deras. Subsequently, the affiliation begins and one starts internalizing the fact that one has to get into the hijra home sooner or later. But they have different patterns for their recruitment as per the description given by them only.

Case 4, having led some life at her original home, explained,

"It was a time when I was to decide about my life. Two conflicting thoughts used to occur, time and again. One, since people living around know my identity, should I continue to live with my widow mother ? Two since the hijras also take away a hijra, can I expect to live with my mother for ever ? Ever since I became conscious of my being sexually unusual, I had started knowing about hijras. This little knowledge led me to leave my home and go to a town in Punjab where a male hijra was living. I touched his feet and told him about my sexual identity. That hijra at first showed some reluctance. He raised certain questions about my whereabouts then he sent another chela of his to validate my information by visiting my home town. Though I was permitted to stay in the hijra home yet my acceptance came later when the Guru had satisfied himself by collecting all the necessary information about me."

Case 8, who came down to Punjab at the age of eighteen and started living as a woman, faced a large number of difficulties especially due to language problem. Inability to communicate with others created isolation for her. She narrated,

"I could hardly talk with anyone. From Punjab, I went to Dehradun where I learnt that a Tamilian hijra was living there. I started searching for him. One day, I saw a group of three hijras passing through the bazaar. I started following them. After passing some distance, one of the hijras questioned me as to why I was following them. I told them that I was looking for a hijra from Tamil Nadu living in Dehradun. I was told by them that the Tamilian hijra was their Guru. I was taken before him. I started narrating to him in Tamil that I had been desperately moving from one place to another in search of peace. The Guru responded by saying that I would get peace only when I die. He however, admittted me into the home provisionally. I was told that the initiation will take place only when some of the hijras living in the nearby towns come and bless the new comer."

Case 18 explained,

"At that time my age was only 10 years and I had come to know what was wrong with me. Since the children of my age would never play with me, I used to roam purposelessly. One day, a Sunday morning, I was going towards the fields when I saw a hijra going with two men having harmonium and Dholki. The hijra, in particular, was wearing shining clothes. They were talking loudly laughing and cutting sexually charged jokes at each other. I enjoyed their talks. It attracted me a lot and I thought that I could be happy only if I join them. That day, instead of going back home, I went after them. From a close quarter I watched them carefully. I also started imitating them. They reached their home and went in. The house was pretty and quite big. I did not go in but was trying to sing and dance like them in front of their home. A man with drak face and ugly looks saw me and then came down to me. He asked me my name and then holding my arm took me inside the home. He put off all clothes. It frightened me and I started crying. There were eight hijras living in that home. All of them assembled there. Then one of them, who was quite elderly, took me in her arms, embraced me, kissed my head and after making me me sit in her lap, said that I was her daughter. I should not fear anything. In the evening they brought *sharab* (whisky) and meat. They celebrated my entry into their group. Songs were sung. The head of that home was congratulated. I was given a *chunni*, a gold chain to put around my neck and a promise was taken from me that I shall never leave them. From that day onward, I have been a professional hijra."

A brief reference to the pattern of voluntary recruitment brings in view many important dimensions. The first dimension being provisional recruitment (e.g. case 4 and 8 show it). A question, why provisional recruitment is made, may be asked here. The reason for making temporary affiliation is that the head of a hijra home wants to make sure that the newcomer does not have any dispute with any other hijra of the region. Also, if a hijra has already been working under some other head hijra then there can be serious disputes between the two heads of Deras. As it shall be seen later in the section on organization, there exists a code of conduct for the hijras in the matters concerning recruitment, etc.

The second notable aspect is the age factor. Those, who join at a relatively younger age, can be admitted straight away (e.g. case 8). This has a relation with the first dimension because the possibilities of disputes and other kind of crises are more in the case of grown up cases than the younger ones. The third aspect refers to the linguistic and regional background which play an important role in the acceptance of a hijra for recruitment (e.g. case 8). Another, the fourth aspect deals with the looks of a hijra. A hijra with a beautiful face is considered as an aspect to the Dera. It was noticed that even the hijras do not mind paying for the purchase of such a case (e.g. case 16). The fifth dimension involves celebrations following recruitment of the new members.

Besides the above referred to dimensions there is one very interesting case whose motivations and consequent recruitment had entirely been different than all other cases studied for the present work. It is case 7 who is not a born hijra but who later got castrated to become a hijra. Before going into the details of this case it is desirable to mention that the practice of castration had been quite popular since the times of Righveda (see, chapter on history of hijras). In the recent times, this practice has come to be regarded as cruel and undesirable in the society at large and by certain sections of the hijras also. Lately, a news appeared in *The Tribune* (deted 13 October 1986) which stated that 0,000 young boys between the age of 15 years and 20 years get castrated every year and become the members of 11 lakh hijra empire. Why do they become so? It is in relation to this question that the researcher considers it worthwhile to discuss case 7.

The case in reference is a huge, ugly looking, middle aged hijra and comes from a poor scheduled caste family of a town in Punjab. The primary occupation of his parents was that of sweepers and scavengers. Born as a normal boy, Prem (his name) went to school and studied upto fifth class. He could not continue his education due to poor economic conditions of the family. This was certainly against the will as he wanted to become something and to own things such as a bicycle, a transistor, etc. These things used to be the possession of a few economically better off. But his dreams shattered. Since, usually economic and occupational heritage perpetuates, he started following his parental occupation. The return in this occupation was carrying head loads of night soil, dirt of people's homes and few rupees. Prem, while recollecting his past days, was laughing just to give way to his anguish over the drudgeries he had once faced. He talked about the way he was castrated and admitted into the hijra home. He told,

> "A day was fixed for my castration. Two old hijras from a distant place also arrived for this occasion which is rather an occasion marked by gaiety and celebration. This is considered as a rebirth of an individual. The preparations were made. A new red-coloured suit was got stitched for me. The day came. A doctor was called. He cut my genitals by operating upon me. He charged Rs. 1000/-as his fee. The act was kept secret. In the evening there was a feast. A goat was cut. Bottlesof liquor were opened. They all drank, danced and offered *Badhai* to my Guru. Thus, I became what I am today. The greed of money and desire to become rich made me so."

The foregoing narration made by case 7 reveals two very significant aspects concerning recruitment and motivation to get recruited. One, that it is the desire to acquire sufficient assets which makes one to become a member of the hijra home and which possibly must have been the case with many who get themselves castrated. Two, even if one is not a born hijra one can become so by way of getting oneself castrated. The later aspect, however, gives rise to certain fundamental questions of interest. First, is the practice of castration acceptable in the contemporary times? Second, does, any other way, apart from the operation as was seen in case 7, exist for the castration reflecting more upon the recruitment through such means?

With respect to first question it may be argued that such a practice is inhumanitarian. Nevertheless, it had existed in the past in an institutionalized form. Its rationalization and legitimization was done on the basis of various pretexts like a form of punishment. However, it proved functional to kings and ruling class and, thus, continued to exist. It has also been observed in the section dealing with historical aspect of hijras. In the contemporary times, it is illegal but still continues because many of the Gurus procure young boys and get them castrated. A recent news item in a daily newspaper contained some resentment towards such a practice. Mr. Kharaiti Lal Bhola, Head of all India Hijra Kalyan Sabha submitted a memorandum to Prime Minister, Rajiv Gandhi. Mr. Bhola said, "Gurus of the eunuch empire were responsible for the castrations...98 per cent of the eunuchs were castrated males. True hermaphrodites were very rare and, therefore, there was no question of over 11 lakh population of them in the country." Why do they get young males castrated? On this question, Mr. Bhola stated, "Some groups of eunuchs collect hundreds of rupees every day and deposit the amount with their Gurus, who in return, pay them Rs. 15 a day. They are treated as bonded labour and rebellion from any group was crushed by the powerful Gurus." This explanation makes obvious the motivation of heads of the hijra homes. They, in a bid to maximize their earnings, recruit young boys and get them castrated. This tendency of the Gurus perpetuates the hijra cult and, thus, carries out recruitments. The exploitative nature of relationships betwcen *Guru* and his *chelas* can be better understood in the forthcoming chapter on hijra organization. It may, however, be stated that this practice of castration is accepted by many due to various economic motives but condemned only by few, who are, in fact, born hijras.

With regard to ways of castration, it may be stated that there had been a number of ways through which castrations had been taking place in the Indian and other world societies, especially those where the practice of castration was quite popular. The most primitive method prevailed in the from of crushing of testicles. The evidence to this practice comes from Atharvaveda. Similarly, testicles were cut as per the description available in Vedic texts. This was done due to various reasons, as has already been referred to in the section on historical past of the hijras. Apart from these two methods, there have been castrations inspired by religion and rituals. The example of Galii, the priests of Cybela, the mother goddess, indicates self-castration to secure chastity. In this respect it has been observed,

> "Wrought up to the highest pitch of religious excitement, the galli dashed the several portions of themselves against the image of the cruel goddess. These broken instruments of fertility were afterwards reverently wrapt up and buried in the earth."[11]

Similarly, those who castrated themselves in honour of the Syrian Astarte of Hierapolis, "after performing the mutilation upon themselves ran through the city carrying in their hands the severed parts." [12] In this way, historical evidences show that castration had been a legitimate practice and was carried out in different ways.

In the contemporary times, according to the respondents' account, and an evidence, from an article it is evinced that castration is a ritual among the hijras. Before its performance, the person on whom it has to be performed is purified by giving him a bath and new clothes, mostly a red coloured suit or sari.

According to a case in Salunke's article reported in *Illustrated Weekly of India* (8 August 1976), the following procedure was adopted. A hijra explains :

> "I was lifted by four hijras and put on a heap of ashes. They held me tight, while the rest (of the hijras) kept on singing and dancing in the adjoining hall. The drumbeats now rose to a frenzy. The old hijra came to me and seized my genitals with his left hand, and with his right hand, slit the bamboolath in the centre, running it down quite close to my pubis. The slit firmly held my genital at the root. The burly hijra ran down his sharp razor along the face of the lath and removed my penis, testicles and scrotum in one swoop, leaving a large bleeding wound. Soon another hijra poured boiling oil to stanch the bleeding. The wound was covered with a rag soaked in warm oil."[13]

Such practices though legitimate ones in the hijra community, however, are illegal according to the laws of the society. Since it is a part of their socio-culural life it goes unchallenged barring little opposition coming from some quarters.

After having discussed the voluntary recruitments and also some of the practices associated with it, specifically that of castration, the case of forced recrùitments may be discussed here. Its necessity arises as there are 6 such cases (no. 1,3,10, 14,15 and 17). While case 1 and 3 were recruited in their infancy, the others were, however, recruited when they had crossed the age of six years. The case history analysis of these cases brought into limelight that having got recruited in their infancy they themselves did not know anything. Their respective Gurus, however, informed the researcher that these hijras' parents put some resistance in handing over their hijra children to them. On the question what way the resistance was put, they stated, "the members of the panchayats were asked to pursue the Gurus to take some money in lieu of them. But a hijra belongs to hijras, so there was no question of any leniency. Even some of the females in the village wept in sympathy but that too could not deter the hijras in making their demand". The real version of forced or coerced recruitment, however, comes from case No. 10,14,15 and 17, who stayed with their own families for a time period exceeding six years. At those ages of theirs they were fully conscious about what happened with them.

Case 10 narrated that he was running 11th year of his age when one day a group of hijras visited his parents' home. According to him,

> "On seeing them my parents asked me to hide myself in the adjoining room. I immediately did so. The hijras were requesting my parents to hand over me to them. But my parents would not concede to their demand. After fifteen-twenty minutes' exchange of arguments, both the parties started shouting loudly. The hijras said that I being of neither sex belonged to them only. It was a custom upheld for centuries. The whole thing went up till late midnight. My mother cried helplessly. My father tried to scare away them with threats of dire consequnces. But all that went in vain. Finally, I had to leave the house. Though, my mother used to visit me in my Dera yet she was not in favour of my staying there. One day, after a year's time, I asked my parents not to come there. This was how I departed and you can imagine how painful was the whole affair."

Same way the cases 14 and 15 were forced to leave their parents' homes. Case 17, however, had to undergo more trouble than case 10, 14 and 15.

Case 17 was well protected, loved and liked by his parents. But the problem in his case started when his elder brother and sister started envying him because of two reasons. First, he was loved so much by his parents that, at times, it amounted to tension between his parents and brother and sister. Second, his brother and sister used to have very tough time in their peer-groups and in the schools. The other children used to discriminate against them because of their hijra brother. And many a time many embarrassing questions were put. All these led to his recruitment as per the narration by the hijra himself,

> "One day my brother and sister got very angry with me. My brother informed the hijras about me. They came to take me. The news spread in the whole village. Everybody assembled outside our home. There were 15 hijras who had come there. They were shouting, abusing and even became violent. The police was called. The village sarpanch was persuaded to put pressure upon hijras to withdraw their demand. But all that could not work. Finally, the police intervened. My parents agreed to give me to them. Thus, I got into hijra cult unwillingly. Even after my joining I could not adjust. One day I got a chance to get away from them. It was a mela in a nearby city. In the rush I disappeared. From Layallpur (in Pakistan) I reached Lahore. At the time of partition, I came down to Amritsar. There I started leading the life of an ordinary labourer. But I could not adjust there. From there, I came to Ambala. At Ambala I was spotted by a hijra. He took me to his home. But I escaped from there at night and reached Patiala. After reaching Patiala, I was too tired to run here and there. I was again in the nets of hijras. Though I have been now living here for quite a long time, yet I have not danced even a single time. I only play *Dholak* whenever we go out. I still feel sometimes that I should run away from here. But the society, circumstances and the hijras continue to force me to live here."

The cases pertaining to forcible recruitment tend to suggest that is it not always the hijras themselves who force a hijra to join them but sometimes the family members, due to various interests, drive them out. It happened in the case of case.[17]

Besides the above discussed two types of ways of recruitment, the foregoing also tends to suggest that recruitment to hijra cult is, by and large, socially conditioned. Wherever, the analyses have shown voluntary recruitment, it in fact has been a case of forced recruitment. The individual motivations, however, only develop when the society rejects them. Nevertheless, the whole set of circumstances is one of the most crucial aspects which accounts for one more step forward in the institutionalization of a non-normal role.

3.3 Socialization and Role Taking

The foregoing section dealt with the patterns of recruitment of hijras into hijra home. It was found that the recruitment process involved two modes, namely the voluntary and coercive. Following which the next issue of vital concern arises as to how the new recruits, especially those who have been recruited through the use of coercion, get themselves adjusted within the hijra community and adapt themselves to a set up which happens to be entirely different from normal households. Secondly, how are the recruits perceived by the already living inmates of hijra homes ? Thirdly, how the relationships between the already living inhabitants of hijras' home and the new recruits get established ? This question has a special reference to those who are grown ups and have been recruited through coercive means. All these questions basically pertain to one major issue as to how such recruits institutionalize the hijra way of life ? A spontaneous answer to such questions could be that with the passage of time in the new setting one is able tn internalize the values. Such an answer though is quite relevant yet the internalization of values is not simply the outcome of one's living in a specific environment but it is the result of a long drawn process which moulds individuals to adopt a specific way of life. Also, as the case histories and circumstances leading to recruitment suggest the recruitment is not just a value free action but a value loaded decision taken by hijras after due considerations and rational thinking. In view of this it is, therefore, essential to analyse what is it that makes the new recruits adopt the hijra way of life.

The institutionalization of a role and legitimization of any specific type of way of life is not possible without socialization, a process which has considerable bearing on the learning of a role by individuals concerned. In general, the proposition holds that the process of socialization is significant in learning a role. In the context of the present study, however, it has a very vital role, especially with regard to the assimilation of hijras with a new and unified way of life since they come from diverse socio-economic, cultural, ethnic, regional and religious settings. Following the expected cruciality of socialization the present section attempts at analysing how this process transforms young recruits into professional hijras.

The field explorations concerning different dimensions of hijras' socialization and their subsequent development revealed that immediately after their recruitment the inmates of the hijras' home begin with teaching the new-comers about the ways, mannerism and other values, like obedience, which form an essential part of code of conduct* of the hijra organization. While the emphasis upon the value of 'obedience' suggests that repressive spcialization seems to be the dominant mode, yet it is worth mentioning that functional and utilitarian aspects remain predominant in the total process of socialization**. These aspects are involved in the operation mainly for the purpose of making an individual feel at home and, therefore, make socialization difficult. Thus, gifts in the form of new clothes, sweets, good food and various other things of individual's choice are presented to a newcomer. The function and utility of such gifts is basically measured in terms of the degree to which an acceptance is expressed by the new hijra recruit. Moreover, such gifts prepare new recruits to participate voluntarily in the process of socialization. It is, therefore, quite appropriate to put forth here that the main

*Code of conduct shall be dealt with in detail in the chapter on Social Organization of Hijras.

** The functional and utilitarian aspects in the context of hijras' socialization refer to that kind of behaviour on the part of the elders through which they are able to gain for the total hijra community.

cherished mode of socialization, seemingly, is not repressive but participatory as the latter ensures a smooth bringing up.

Notwithstanding the mode of socialization adopted, the authority of the Guru in the teaching process is supreme and unchallengeable. The unchallengeable aspect of Guru's authority is Guru's position which is legitimized by the total hijra community. The Guru is always an elderly man whose Guruship is solemnized publically. Only the panchayat of hijras has the authority to challenge any Guru of a Dera. The chelas do not have any power as such. A 90 year old female hijra from Orissa heading a hijra Dera at Patiala consisting of 8 members narrated the following in the context of her authority and socialization :

"The Guru in a Hijra Home is Mother of all the inmates. Mother has the right to guide and govern her children. All the inmates are my children and, therefore, my authority is above all the members. Moreover, *Gaddi* (seat) of Guru was not simply got through ageing but this was granted to me by the earlier head on account of my fitness to become Guru. It is, therefore, my moral duty to manage the affairs of the Home in a dedicated manner. It is also my duty to see that all the members live in harmony, follow the division of labour as decided by me in consultation with other members and learn the art of clapping, dancing, singing, begging, according to the instructions imparted by me."

With regard to the mode of socialization, the Guru told,

"*Dekhna parta hai ki bachcha kacha hai ya pacca* (It is to be judged whether the child is soft or a hard one in the context of learning). Accordingly, the method is decided. If the child is soft, agreeable and obedient in learning, the child is offered good clothes, shown movies and taken out of the Dera for enjoyment. These are the motivating rewards. The child is, therefore, moulded to perform in the way expected from hijras. The method of teaching with rewards as motivating factors does work and bring about the fruits. But then all the five fingers of a hand are not equal. What I mean to say is that among the recruits there are good as well as some Maskhra (naughty) ones In such a situation the proverb 'spare the rod spoil the child' is given a serious thought. Thus, the use of rod is also made to bring to book any such persons. *Kyonki Laton ke Bhoot Baaton Se Nahin Mante, isi liye danda ka istemal jruri ho jata hai* (since it is not easy to get the things done by verbal order, therefore, the use of stick becomes essential)."

Besides love and affection bestowed on new recruits by Guru in socializing them, it is also obvious from the above that the occasional use of stick is also made and that it helps in making the new recruit adapt himself to new environment. The mode of socialization, therefore, also depends upon the type of recruit under consideration. The information collected from the case histories also suggests that the socialization of a child recruit is easier than the socialization of the adult recruit. The basic reason for this is that in the childhood learning begins with first exposure to everything. The child, being in the process of developing his abilities, picks up everything easily. Thus, learning in the case of child newcomer is easier. But when the individual is grown up, he has so much of exposure to various objects and people that he has already got certain fixed notions about things and phenomena. That is why in the socialization of adults the first step is brain-washing exercise and then second learning. The Guru further explained :

"*Bacha to mom ke saman hota hai. Jaisa aap chaho use dhal sakte hain* (The child is like wax, one can mould him the way one likes). My experience of Guruship is now about thirty five years. During this period all these people living here were recruited. Some of them just in their childhood. When they came here as children, that time they did not know who they were, who were their parents and where they were living prior to their entry into Hijra Home. In few days' time they picked up the style of living of this Dera. They were taken out by the elder inmates to the houses of others. The dance, glittering clothes and similar objects, received by them as gifts, used to be so attractive for them that when they retired for the day and came back home they could be seen dancing and singing. What I mean to say is that *mahol* (environment) helps them pick up the way of life. One does not require a special effort. By the time the young ones grow they are already transformed into full-fledged hijras".

The details about how environment helps the young ones is their socialization were further supplemented by the accounts given by Kamla, case 3, when she said,

"I was barely five years old when I was brought to this Hijra Dera by my Guru from my parents. In the new home everything looked strange to me. The people who were addressed as uncles in the home became aunties when they went out of the home. These males used to call dirty abuses (at that time these seemed dirty to me but now these are a part of daily life), drank liquor and smoked cigarettes but when they went out of home they behaved like females and did not use any dirty language with any lady in the outside society. However, everybody loved me, brought eatables for me, sent me to shop to fetch them cigarettes and in the process I almost forgot my previous home. The Guru of my Dera took special care of me. She taught me the first lesson in clapping and dancing. Next was how to perform dance at someone's place and to beg *Badhai* (expected reward on congratulating a householder). Gradually, while acting and interacting with the inmates of the Dera and also with guest hijras I became familiar with the customs and norms of the hijras. I took great interest in learning everything and as a result, at the age of thirteen years I was as learned as my senior colleagues were in the profession (*dhanda*). The day came when my Guru made me the bride and started sending me for work. The first dance* which I performed as a professional was at the residence of a Zamindar in the nearby village. I was good looking, young and attractive, the Zamindar was impressed by my performance. Besides *Badhai*, I was given a prize of Rs. 100/-and a gold ring. This was my great achievement and it earned me a good reputation among the fellow hijras. But I had to shift from that place after some time. Once a Panchayat (congregation) of hijras was held where I was asked to perform dance for elders of the hijra community. An old head of a hijra *sthan* (home) at Ludhiana bought me there and then only' I had to shift but it effected me very much. But that is the life we are supposed to live."

The foregoing narration depicts a case of complete conformity to the desires of the elders on the part of some of the hijras on the one hand and trouble free learning through participatory method on the other. What is significant to note here is a trouble-free learning which, according to most of them, is always the case. The enquiries also bring into focus certain stray cases having a troublesome socialization and, therefore, maladjustment. Case 13, who looks very ugly with protruding teeth explained the way he was trained right from his childhood days by the Guru of the Dera and other inmates. By scratching his forehead, Rattu, the case under consideration, tried to recollect facts of his childhood training by delving deep into his memory lanes,

Bibi (mother), an old lady whose physical appearance was partly that of a male and partly of a female was God for me. I remember only her who used to address me as *put* (son). It often made me wonder that when I was addressed as son why should I then be given female clothing to put on and taught to learn the habits of females. Likewise, other members of the Dera who were fullfledged men always remained in female garbs. The use of vulgar gestures was

*The hijra dance is not a specialized dance based on any classical rhythm. They simple move round and clap on the tune of a popular film song.

the major source of entertainment for all these people. I remained among them and, therefore, started finding myself comfortable with the said style of life. In fact, my seniors would often ask me to say *Gali* (abuses) and I therefore, learnt all vulgarity in my early childhood days. Now I understand why, as a child, I was often made to share bed with these hefty men of the Dera. They would often fiddle with me by kissing and stripping me off, hugging and fingering deep into me. Whenever I resented, I was told that one had to live through all this. *Koi aurat nahin aiyegi yahan, aapas mein hi kaam chalana parta hai* (no female will come here, we have to manage ourselves). This was the beginning and now I also do the same whenever we have a child hijra with us."

The description put forth by Rattu is an indication to the fact that how certain experiences of an individual prove to be too much in the process of learning. The early life experiences of homosexual activities had further implications in his adjustment and inter-relationship with other fellow hijras. Rattu smiled and continued,

"What else could we do. Nothing! However, these were the things which made me learn how to pass sexual obvertures towards others in the public. No inhibitions no *sharam* (shame)...*sab chalta hai* (everything is fair). But, besides all this I learnt dancing, singing, clapping and stripping off in public to show my anger. Initially, I went out as a helper with the elder ones, carried load of atta (flour) and other eatables and any other material on my head which was earned throughout the day. Since I was taught all bad things by my elders in the beginning, I became very mischievous and, therefore, would play traunt, land into serious troubles, bear the scoldings and, therefore, became adamant. Some of these habits I have even now."

Rattu became serious with gloom all over his face, started abusing his elders for whatever they did to him in his childhood. With some anger he said,

"Something did go wrong in my case. I was loved by all the inmates when I performed all sorts of chores for them. But whenever I tried to play with the kids in the Basti (locality) I was disallowed. If ever, I went out I made use of abuses and dirty remarks which made me unwanted outside the Dera. Often the kids would beat me. When I came back into Dera, crying, with torn-off clothes, I was subjected to punishment which included solitary confinement, starvation and beatings. All that made me stubborn and also spoiled my relations with others. This is the reason why even today I am dis-respected among the people of my biradari (community). About two years back, I was shunted out of my Guru's residence. I was wrongly charged with the allegation that I had stolen the purse and gold ornaments of the Guru. As a consequence of which my relations with the members of my community have been severed except for with few personal friends."

As a matter of fact some enquiries made from other hijras whom Rattu claims as his friends, reveal that he (Rattu) in fact is a very mischievous person. The panchayat which decided his expulsion from his Guru's house did it on the basis of his admittance of the crime committed by him. The elderly hijra. who presided over this panchayat said, "It is unfortunate that such a thing has happened. But the guilty has to be punished. Actually the fault is his Guru's who did not teach him properly right from the beginning". It is therefore, worth mentioning here that the result of improper socialization can be bad, as it is obvious from the case of Rattu. It may be further argued that Rattu is not the only case of a spoiled type but one can find many who, because of their wrong socialization, have been made to suffer throughout their life. The case of Jethu, another hijra, is worth presenting here to highlight the problems emerging out of wrong socialization.

Jethu, a 70 year old hijra with wrinkled face, physically very weak and sick has been found living in miserable conditions. Uncared by his community, Jethu is leading a lonely life. His existing conditions give rise to a very significant question, why is it that while most of the hijra Gurus have built up their houses and occupy Gaddis, this fellow is living in acute poverty and isolation ? A number of questions pertaining to his present state were raised with a view to exploring the reasons for his pitiabie living conditions. The responses to these questions, however centered around the events which took place in the past. The following excerpts from the discussion explain the story,

> "What should I say ? The situation in which I am today is the consequence of what happened many years back. I was brought up more by hijras than my own parents. The environment in the Dera was such that I could never think beyond what I saw and experienced through my interaction with others. All those years divided my life into two settings. One, a formal setting in which I was asked to learn the art of clapping in hijra style, take to dancing and singing on the tune of some songs played on harmonium by a person called Chacha (uncle) by everyone in the Dera. I was then ten years old. The hijra way of life certainly impressed and effected me. I was gradually moulded into it. But in the beginning it was difficult to follow whatever I was taught by my elders. Very often I made mistakes and each mistake was followed by a slap on my face. I remember, the impact of the slap was so strong that I could even feel the impression of the hand on my face. Obviously, I cried. But always I was either asked to stop crying through the shouts by the head of the household or I got more slaps on my face. After that the whole day used to pass in solitude, hunger, thirst and whatever can be as misery for a helpless lad of 10 years".

The respondent who was lying on the bed got up and started saying further,

> "Sometimes many days passed like that. I starved. If I picked up certain habits of behaving like hijras, there was no encouragement except for the remark of my Guru,

such as *Kaise nahin sikhega, iska baap bhi sikhega. Kaun khilayega isko jawaiyon ki tarah*' (How will he not learn ? Even his father will learn. Who will feed him as a son-in-law)*. Such remarks would irritate me. I would often abuse my Guru. You can imagine what happened then—beatings with sticks. As a part of punishment I was asked to clean utensils, sweep the house, go to market to fetch wheat flour, weighing 20 to 30 kgs, on my head. All this hampered my learning and filled me with a sense of hatred towards hijras. I could not learn the art of dancing and begging Badhai throughout my life. I started hating hijras, their attitudes and behaviour. Since I could not be thrown out of the Dera under the rules of hijra community, the emphasis shifted from singing and dancing to learning of harmonium (popularly referred to as Peti). I was a failure in that too. I was fifteen years old when my Guru died. The new Guru was a different natured person. He tried to tempt me with all kinds of motivations but nothing made me work. I could learn only beating of drum. Thus, throughout my life, I played the drum whenever we went out to anyone's residence. It was exactly at the age of fifteen and a half that I first accompanied my seniors and thereafter I did the same job for nearly forty years. But my irritable and crude behaviour, which I acquired during the early years of life, very often brought me into confrontation with others. Even now this type of behaviour on my part makes me the most unwanted person among my colleages".

He paused for a moment and thinking aloud put a question to himself, "Why am I lying alone today" ? Answering his own thoughts, he said,

"It is the result of that old hijra who taught me only to fight with others. I tried to change myself a lot but just

* In accordance with the Indian way of life, a son-in-law is highly respected and given special treatment

could not. The habits once formed are hard to change. I experienced insults, abuses, beatings and hard time. I, therefore, like and enjoy being. I like to see others suffer. I had a vast territory to operate which I seized from my Guru. I was outcast by the Biradari. I did not bother. I continued to go in the area of my Guru. If anyone ever obstructed me I paid back in the same manner. The result of all that is that no one wishes to be with me. Whatever money and ornaments I possessed, I sold for my medicine and livelihood. I have no money, nothing which I can call my own. I am totally shattered. I experienced many ups and downs in my life. But one may do good or bad, the end of the life of a hijra is always pathetic, full of sorrow and lots of problems. And I may tell you that as long as these hijras think that one is able to offer them meat and liquor, they are friends, even if insulted and driven out of home. They do not mind all this. But the moment they find that one is penniless, they become arch enemies. Only a few years ago many of them used to spend days and nights here but now when I am in need of someone to care for me, look after me, they do not even pass by my home.

The narrations made by some of the cases, specifically those who were recruited in the early years of childhood, depict participatory socialization on the one hand and repressive socialization on the other result into the making of two different types of individuals with entirely different types of personality. No doubt, in both the cases adaptation to hijra way of life is the ultimate result but adjustment with the said way of life differs significantly from case to case. There is no denying the fact, as also expressed by some Gurus as well as some disciples, that socialization is not a simple process. It being a very difficult and complicated process requires utmost care. It is more so when the individual is recruited against his will. The excessive use of repressive methods hinders this process rather than facilitating it. But again depends more on the person incharge of socialization.

In some cases Ustads (the teacher) did use repressive methods but at the same time an attempt was always made to involve the newcomer so that he ultimately accepted the new way of life. The following description provided by case 14 reveals that much depends upon, when, where and to what extent repressive as well as participatory methods are used to brain-wash a person and then mould him according to the desired way of life. The respondent narrated his own experience by saying,

> "As far as I am able to recall, it was indeed a great time. I was under the charge of a male hijra who was next to Guru. The Guru instructed him that there should not be any problem to me. However, it is also important to mention that Guru gave strict instructions, from time to time, for my training and bringing up. I was asked to put on female garbs, dance and sing. Initially I was not able to pick up. I was shy. I had inhibitions. Sometimes, I would not act according to instructions. Then Guru used to call me by his side and tell me that sooner or later I must pick up this *dhanda* (occupation) as it is going to be my bread and butter. At times, Guru did show his anger and scolded me but never gave any beatings. The Guru took me to other Deras where I was shown how everyone acts and behaves. All this made me familiar with customs, beliefs and other attributes associated with my pressnt occupation."

The researcher was further apprised of by the same respondent about how he stepped into performing the occupation duties. He said,

> "When I was somewhat aware of what I was supposed to do, my Guru asked me to accompany his other chelas for the work. I, alongwith others, used to visit people's houses. My senior colleagues taught how to approach a household especially the ladies and then insist upon giving a performance. Once I was asked by colleagues to dance, I was not able to do. Then another colleague of mine said, she is our

Bobby and feels shy. On listening the remark the ladies gathered around and laughed. Then my colleague caught my hand and started dancing. After five minutes I could pick up the rhythm. That was the beginning. After few visits with my colleagues, my Guru allotted me an area in which I was asked to go and operate independently. I started going with a harmonium player and a drum beater. My companions used to sing songs from Hindi movies or local folks in Punjabi and I used to dance. That way, I started earning my bread and now there is no looking back. All credit goes to my Guru and my seniors in the Dera who made me what I am today."

The foregoing analysis, based primarily upon the vivid versions of how they were socialized, brings into view one conclusive result that what type of personality of a hijra is going to develop, depends upon how one is socialised. As it has been seen through the foregoing accounts, both types of socialization techniques, the repressive and participatory, are used by the heads of the hijra homes to socialize their disciples. The success or failure in learning, adjustment or maladjustment with the role and other members in the hijra's home, poverty and prosperity or to say everything, to a very large extent, depends upon the way one is brought up. The environment of hijra's home is very crucial in the attitude and habit formation and in making an individual conformist or deviant. The cases cited above also reflect upon the type of socialization and role taking by the other hijras interviewed by the researcher. In fact, a large number of hijras have conforming attitude and there are rare ones who grow up as some sort of deviant characters within the hijra community.

Furthermore, it is also a question of interests of the hijra, in general, and of Guru, in particular, to see that the new recruits get adjusted well. The reason, which the hijras cited for such an interest, is that if a hijra does not get adjusted in hijra biradari then he cannot adjust anywhere. Most of the Gurus try that their chelas should respect and regard them. On the other hand, it is a question of getting regular earning by the Guru as well as the chela. This, in fact, is one of the most crucial motives of both the Guru and the chela. It is a question of their survival. Since both cannot find any other alternative to have regular income the perpetuation of the hijra cult becomes an inevitable choice. This is done through recruitment, socialization and role-taking. This is partially an explanation of how the chelas act as economic feeders to the Guru. Though this aspect will be discussed later yet to add here for information that according to the descriptive accounts provided by the respondents it is found that all the chelas deposit their day-to-day's earnings with the Guru. There is a general pool where all the chelas of a Dera pool their earnings—cash as well as in kind. Then the major share is taken by the Guru to run the affairs of the Dera. The remaining money is distributed among chelas as their pocket money and for meeting certain specific expenses. The Guru and the disciples in a Dera at Patiala discern that when all of them come back home from routine Pheri (visits), all the nine of them deposit whole of their earnings including cash, clothes, eatable material, etc. with the Guru. Fifty per cent of the cash is distributed by the Guru among all his disciples, twenty per cent is given to Dholkiwala who is normally a non-hijra and the remaining thirty per cent is kept by the Guru. The eatables etc. are utilized by them in their routine life. The clothes are kept by the Guru who distributes these among his disciples whenever they demand and need. The daily income of the Dera ranges between Rs. 400 to Rs. 500, depending upon the Badhai. Thus, the Guru is able to keep around Rs. 100 to Rs. 200 a day. This is a handsome amount which obviously is the major attraction for most of the Gurus. It is, therefore, in this way that the young hijras are recruited and who subsequently become economic feeders of the Gurus. For the chela the money is not only a source of livelihood but through it he makes a place for himself in the hijra community and thus adjusts with others.

In the light of the above discussion, it may be argued that

socialization process, which involves formal and informal training, repressive and participatory methods, etc. enables new recruits to take on the role of hijra. Besides, socialization, certain motivating factors, such as monetary considerations and question of making a living, are also very important in inducing a person for taking up a particular type of role.

3.4 Role Performance: Expectations, Strains and Perpetuation of Role

The foregoing discussion on socialization and role-taking indicated that socialization process has a very significant contribution in learning of role by the hijras. Along with the said the monetary interests of the new comers and that of the heads of hijra homes have also been found to be of crucial significance. Such an indication also gives rise to the need for further exploration into a very relevant issue, that is what after role taking and what are the associated aspects of life after role taking? It is the role performance which begins after the learning of a role.

'Role Performance', in sociological terms, implies an activity of an actor which also has some influence on the other actor involved in the given social situation. When individuals are involved in any activity, precisely in occupational life, according to Worsley[14], there is always some role playing and some recognition of the different expectations of different audience. Since exception of others from the incumbent of a role is an essential aspect it. therefore, also implies that a role is always oriented and performed in relation to others who have some expectations. The said expectations, as Mead[15] would argue, could be seen in the form of certain reactions. According to Mead, role playing involves some kind of reaction from individuals to their own gestures and at the same time anticipate others, behaviour towards themselves, in the same manner. Why do individuals see and anticipate the reflection of their own gestures in the behaviour of others? The basic rationale for this is that each role performance involves mutual expectations of the actors involved in the interaction process. The mutuality of expectations, therefore, also as Nadel[16] would put it, 'is the execution of rights and obligations by individuals in the society'. Nadel's position also comes closer to Goffman[17] who looks at role-performance from the point of view of 'enactment of rights and duties attached with the status of the individual in a given social situation in relation to others. The author, therefore, understands that role performance involves others and rests upon the expectations which others have from the incumbent of that role. At the same time the incumbent of the role may also have some expectations from others. These expectations can also be, at times, seen in terms of exchange of tangible and intangible goods and services. The reason being that in all the occupational areas of life the individuals involved do make cost-benefit analysis.[18] Especially, when the role performer has some type of deficits in his being and for others the same deficits become extremely functional.

Accepting the argument that the role performance involves a social situation and mutual expectations of the actor (who performs the role) and others (who expect the role to be performed in a specific way), the case of the role of hijras in relation to the society at large can now be taken up for analysis. To begin with there are two basic but important questions which need to be considered, first (a) what role a hijra, who is discarded by the society, can play for the society; and (b) what can be the expectations of the society associated with the role of hijra? (c) What are the expectations of a hijra from the society in lieu of his role?

The question of the role which a hijra can play is primarily a historical question and the answer to the same can be found in the history. In the context of historicity of the said role, Chapter 2 (Section 2.1) highlighted the role played by hijras. Accordingly, it was enumerated that the hijras in the Indian as well as middle-eastern society of the past had been playing very significant roles from time to time. At one time they were considered as pious men and, therefore, were elevated to the level worthy of standing at the doors of great mosques in Mecca and their hands were used to be kissed by all those who went inside the mosque. At some other time, they were castrated either for giving punishment or were presented as gifts by one king to another, for they could act as faithful slaves in Persia or Babylon. In Mughal India, they were expected by the kings to safeguard the women in harems by acting as guards. They weie preferred to other men because of their sexual disabilities. In certain cases the kings made them high officials in the military and politics as they were not expected to demand any wealth and intergenerational perpetuation of their offices. The reason being that they could not get married because of their asexuality. Due to this factor they did not have any family and children, thus, no one for whom they required any wealth amassed and office perpetuated. In the modern Indian society, though they do not have civil or military positions, yet again they continue to be functionally very important. They are expected; first, to help a family to avoid stigma as they happily take away any asexual individual; second, they go and bless the male child born in a family or bless the bridegroom's house for a healthy married life and for procreation of male issue. The male issue, as well known, is attached great value in any family especially in the Indian society.

In the light of the foregoing, especially, the role which hijras can perform in the contemporary society, it is, therefore, suggested that the people in the society do have certain expectations from them. Their expectations, however, may differ from individual to individual and class to class. Though it is a difficult thing to assume and also to make any generalization regarding the relationship between class and expectations, yet some accounts based upon author's observations and enquiries with people in general do indicate such a relationship existing to certain extent. There are broadly three types of reactions by people to whenever the hijras go to their houses for the performance of their customary role. One type of reaction reflecting peoples' expectations comes from the higher socio-economic strata of Indian society. According to the discussions held with some such persons it has been found that they have an indifferent attitude towards the role performed by hijra. Some excerpts given below from the interview held with a man at whose place the hijras performed a dance reflect upon the expectations which people belonging to higher socio-economic class have:

Author: What do you think of this custom of dancing of hijras at the birth of a male child or marriage, Sir ?

Man : The time have changed so this practice should go. The reason for my saying so is that these people just exort money by pressurizing.

Author: How did you feel when these people reach your place today?

Man : We tried our best to persuade them for not to do any "naach-gaana" (dancing and singing). But these people insisted upon doing it. After that they demanded Rs. 251/- and a saree or a suit. Under perssure one has to pay them otherwise the people of the locality also see the 'tamasha' (show).

Author: What do you think they should do when they come to someone's place?

Man : They should act according to the wish of the resident and should not insist upon dancing. After all their dancing or not dancing hardly makes any difference.

Author: Since they live on this custom only, do you think they can agree easily?

Man : What I mean is that they should simply come, beg and go. But they should not trouble the family and demand too much money. The government should ban this type of custom and give these people work according to their abilities.

The excerpts from the conversation indicate that these people are unwanted among the people of higher socio-economic class. The custom of dancing of a hijra on certain occasions does not fit into the value structure of the people of higher socio-economic strata. But on the contrary, the middle class, especially the lower middle class has a very different attitude. Similar questions were raised to a man of lower middle class,who replied,

"Sab kudrat de rang ne. Koi annah, koi langarạ, te koi na aadmi te na janani. Inha da te ehi kam hai. Is karke inhan nun kise tranh tang nahin karna chahida. Asin te ehi kehnde haan ke eh log te aapna kam karan jo kuchh inha lena hai len te chale jaan". (It is all the will of God that some are blind, cripple or without any sex. It is their profession, therefore, we should not trouble them. We want that they should come and do their job, take whatever they want and then go).

In view of the said arguments what one finds is that they are accepted by people in general especially because of two things. One, that they are the victims of nature, and two, that their custom is conceived as desirable among the people belonging to lower middle class. However, what one does not find is any mythological justification regarding the asexuality of hijra put forward by the people to whom the researcher happened to talk. However, that does not mean the absence of myths and socio-cultural beliefs about hijras in the society. There are a number of mythological beliefs existing about them if one comes down to lower strata of Indian society. According to some field work notes based on author's observations and discussions with people belonging to lower stratum, the following major beliefs can be stated as existing:

(a) "the hijras are very powerful people because of their asexuality. Potent or normal males lose viriya (semen) which hijras do not lose, therefore, all their energies are preserved and, therefore, they are physically powerful people."

(b) "a hijra is born as a symbol of God, it is, therefore, advised that people should not trouble or tease them. The teasing amounts to hurting the feelings and sentiments of hijras. And following which if a hijra curses a man then the man is likely to have a hijra child through his wife."

(c) "blessing by hijra is a boon for the child and the family, for a child acquires great powers and, therefore, does not come under the influences of bhoot-preta (ghosts)".

(d) "whenever a hijra comes to a house he should be given respect and should go back all pleased. A curse of a hijra can ruin the family."

In fact, one can go on adding various beliefs of above types which people have regarding hijras on the one hand and which in return also influence their behaviour and expectations on the other. The reason being that the beliefs have some cultural basis and the relationship between the actors involved in a situation is not only mutually influencing but also guide expectations of each other in the given cultural background.

After having briefly analysed the expectations which people have, vis-a vis, hijra's role in the Indian society, it is now desirable to look at the other aspect of hijra's role, i.e., what are their expectations from the society? Since this part is the most significant from the point of view of the objectives of the study, it is, therefore, essential to make analysis of hijra's expectations at four levels. First, what do they expect from the society in the context of their role? Second, what type of relationship with the society at large is perceived by the hijras themselves? Third, what are the stresses and strains they have in the performance of their role? Fourth, what are the rewards, which in spite of various strains, continue to motivate the hijras for the perpetuation of their role in the society?

Before reflecting upon the expectations of hijras from the society at large, it is significant to bear in mind certain biographical conditions in which hijras live and which guide their entire relationship. Though born of normal human beings, the hijras come into contact with the people in the society only tangentially. In fact, there are only two specific occasions marked by the hijras on which they like to visit people. One, at the occasion of the birth of a male child in a family. Two, at the time of the marriage at bridegroom's place. Since the contact is tangential and interaction, therefore, being limited, the author assumes limited expectations of the hijras from the society at large.

When asked what do they expect from the society, almost all of them stated that since they depend upon their Jajmans (people at whose place they go) for their livelihood, therefore, they only wish happiness of the people. Also whenever they go to people's house they want that they should be given respect like any other human being in the society. To quote case 3, who said,

> "We are also the issues of normal parents. We have also taken birth as any other human being on the earth. We do want to be respected. We respect people, their sentiments and we do help those who are lower to us economically. I am not saying so to praise myself and people in my community. I am telling what is factual. I keep aside 5 per cent of my daily earnings for goodness, "Bahuchare" the "Murgewali Devi". After a year I distribute that money among the poor people in my area as *daan*. I brought up a poor girl and married her to a boy in this locality. On marriage, I spent Rs. 5,000 to Rs. 7,000."

The same case, while pointing towards another girl of 6 years or so of age, said,

"Look at this girl. Her father died when she was hardly

six months old. Her mother is working as cleaner in my Dera. In view of the grim economic conditions of the family and exploitative tendencies among Chuhras (the caste of that girl) I thought of helping the family. I have put this girl into a school. I am helping not because this girl is poor but the thing is that human beings should help each other. We hijras simply spend all our money on liquor. I thought to do a better thing in life so that a good life is insured in the next birth. The way, we think about society, the society should also think with the similar attitude toward us. After all, we are also human beings."

Besides expecting a sympathetic and respectful response from the society at large, the hijras also want the government to consider them as a separate entity of the population of the country. The Constitution of India is silent about the people belonging to middle sex. While explaining what more they expect from people and the state, the case 3 further said,

> "Government ko hamari madad karni chahiya (The government should help us). We are in the society but we are out of the society. We do not have the right to vote. And this amounts to the fact that we are not the citizens of this country. Sahib (Sir) you can imagine what is our status. We want that we should be recognised and returned as hijras in the census. We should have right to vote and we should be given representation on various bodies so that some improvement could be effected in our living conditions our status in the society."

Following the said expressions made by hijras, a question was addressed to them, if they were to be helped by the government, in what way they wished to be helped, how can they reciprocate the help? To this question many answers were given by the respondents. The most important gesture, however, was made by one of them, who said,

"Financially we are in a position to help the government in many small ways. All over India we have our Deras. Each Dera has its territorial jurisdiction. Within that territorial jurisdiction we can buy a small piece of land and donate that for constructing a small school building or Dharamshala or Sarai for the use of people. Similarly, if we are given jobs in offices and institutions, according to our educational qualifications, we can be of some use. But as hijras what we do is nothing."

By and large, as the above excerpts from interviews also suggest, the hijras' expectations revolve around one major issue, that is, their recognition in the society as human beings, as citizens having right to vote and government's intervention to improve upon their status by integrating them with the main stream of the society. They do not wish to live as obscured citizens.

The other question refers to whether their expectations get fulfilled or remain just a wish? Another question related with it is, what type of relationships do hijras have with people in the society? With reference to the said questions, it is worth noting that though hijras' demand for good treatment is a genuine one and they also respect the society, yet it is hard for them, as is obvious from people's reaction to their role, to come across families where they get good treatment. Case 1, who has been in this profession for the last 45 years, when asked about his relations with the members of the society at large, remarked,

"People describe us as worse than dirty drain. What people give us? Money...some eatables...and some clothes... that is all... How do they agree to give us all that...only when we force them...pass some remarks... In their hearts they do not respect us. Can they allow us to enter their homes...sit on the sofa and have a cup of tea, while sitting across each other on a dining table. Never...because they conceive us as inferior human beings... Because they think that we are the worms of dirty drains... Because they have the notion that we are the product of illegitimate union of male and female. I do not care for people. This profession asks us to go to people's place and beg... so I go....I, otherwise hate people".

The respondent, unlike his stout physical appearance and bold locks, broke down while narrating about his acceptance in the society. The respondent apprised the researcher that whenever they go to people's houses, the mischievous children tease them, insult them and sometimes even go to the extent of stoning them in the streets. In such a situation if they react harshly the parents abuse the hijras and ask them why do they come there? While making complaints about the treatment meted out to them the case 1 further said,

> "Hum log to aakhir mein yehi samajhte hain ki logon ke nazron mein hume to gali ke kuta-kuti bhi achhe hain (We finally understand that in people's eyes even a street dog and a bitch are better off than us)".

The case 6 also made it explicit that a hijra is looked down upon in the society. According to her understanding, a hijra is conceived and treated as an untouchable, who is a stigmatized being. Even if a normal human being goes alongwith a hijra in the street the people start doubting the very identity of the former. She posed a challenging question by saying,

> "Let me clad in a pant and shirt, walk with you in the market or street. I am sure, many people will not only stare at me but also at you. They will ask you many questions, such as, what is your relation with the hijra? Even if you give hundred and one justifications they will doubt your integrity not only then but even later on when you are not with me."

The problem of stigma, as noted in the section dealing with identity crisis, not only drive people away from their houses but also continue to haunt them, thus, making their adjustment difficult in the society. The respondents told that even if they go to any public place, their very appearance creates a phobia, a fear of stigma for others. Say, in a cinema theatre, whenever they go, people start laughing and would say.

> "Lo khusre bhi picture dekhan aaye hain" (See, the hijras have also come to see the movie).

Such kind of insulting remarks not only irritate them but also hurt their feelings and they often think that they do not have even the right to watch a movie? Then, one idea gives them consolation that all this is the fruit of their *karma* in the previous birth. They accept it as God's will. As one of the cases remarked,

> "Insaan hijron ki kadar kya karega. Hamein to Bhagwan bhi nahin puchhta (What to talk of men, even God does not bother about us)."

The reason for perceiving such a pathetic kind of relationship with the members of the society by hijras is embodied in the fact that the hijras do not have any constitutional status on the one hand and carry along a sense of stigma generated by the society, on the other. Therefore, their expectations predominantly remain 'good treatment to them by people'. In spite of the fact that the treatment is very often not good, the hijras, however, feel contented as they think they are doing good by going to people's residence and by congratulating them on certain happy occasions. As case 12, talking about her expectations, puts it,

> "We always pray for the happiness of people and in return expect two square meals from them and nothing beyond that. The happiness of the Jajman (host) is our primary consideration.... We do not want to amass money, silver, gold. All this will remain here. If people will remember something they will remember only goodness and not the money. So we do not wish to trouble our jajman upon whom we are to depend for our living. Long live

people and Jajman, we will continue to get food to eat".

Besides the contentment expressed by hijras, they also maintain the superiority of the society over themselves. While the society considers them as outsiders, they continue to respect various policy programmes. For instance, the issue of family planning is directly associated with their profession. A decline in birth rate will mean decline in opportunities for them. Decline in the number of opportunities for them means less earnings. All this seems to be quite upsetting in the case of few. However, most of them exhibit a very positive attitude to such a programme. On the issue of family planning and norm of small family, out of nineteen cases, fifteen cases approved government policy. It is quite appropriate to quote case 11, a Rajput hijra of Himachal Pradesh origin, who said,

> "Most of us live in urban areas where large proportion of the population is educated. The family planning programmes have also become very popular in these areas because of which our earnings have come down considerably. It has affected our expenses and standard of living. The members of our community never used to beg. Now in cities, like Bombay, you can find some of them begging in the streets and markets. It has lowered down our custom... (after a brief pause)... But the society is supreme to us. We do not have any ill-will against family planning programmes...as these are for the larger interests of the society. Look at the children in this colony...they run around uncared by their parents. They do not go to school. How can they go when their parents do not have resources. Why should parents give birth to children when they cannot care for them. The government should have strict rules to reinforce family planning. It will help the country to raise the living standard of people. Once the standard of the country is enhanced we will also have good conditions of living".

It is not only the case 11 who says so. There are others who conform to the policies and programmes of the government. In fact, what they emphasize in the defence of their cult and themselves is not opposed to the larger society. They want respect and wish to reciprocate the same. Though they pass sexual overtures to the onlookers yet barring few stray incidents, they have a respectable attitude towards women in the society. Their basic dealing is with women. Most often, when they visit people's residence they find women at home. They then behave, as told by them, like behaving with a mother or sister. In fact, their behaviour and attiring in female garbs and at the same time they not being females themselves must be creating some type of problems in their dealings with women and, thus, affecting their role performance.

According to the information imparted by the hijras it is found that it is the most difficult thing for them to maintain their relationship with women in the society. The reason being that it is quite upsetting for them. Whenever, they come into contact with women, the first feeling which they have, is "had they themselves been females they would have married someone and given birth to some children." This feeling comes into their mind because of their total socialization process during which they had been trained to act like females. Also, since they put on female garbs and try to pass like females during the time of their role performance the feeling of why they are not actually females does haunt their mind and cause lot of frustration.

Secondly, a hijra has been described as a mischievous character who would very often tease the male folks and pass certain sexual overtures. Sometimes, as the field observations and interviews suggest, most of them do makes use of dirty abuses in their day to day life and dealings with the members of their own community and people who live in the neighbourhood. This habit of their makes it really difficult for them to makes adjustment when they are in the company of females. Though they are successful in behaving in a decent manner, yet it sometimes so happens that hijras do make remarks which amount to some kind of sexual behaviour and exhibitionism. At a dance performance, a hijra talking to a women about her sexual behaviour remarked,

> "Why are you scared of me. I do not have that tool which make you happy at night".

Such type of remarks do reflect vulgarity on the one hand and an embarrassment for the woman confronting the hijra, on the other. Such actions, many of hijras most often approve as normal and a form of expected behaviour, however not without the feeling of guilt. In defence of their such an unexpected behaviour they tell that it is really hard to change, especially when one encounters women in the society. If they do not make use of such actions and overtures then they feel that they have not played their role well. This is, in fact, a real situation where they are in a fix and which involves confflct.

The question, therefore, arises whether passing of sexual overtures is instinctive or it is something through which they try to represent themselves as capable of sexual inter-course. Also whether this is merely a phychological outlet for the release of their suppressed sexual desires and the stresses-strains they have. Another issue related with this is to what extent this affects their role.

In the context of sexual aspect of hijras' life it has been found that they do have feeling of entering into sexual relationship. But their physical condition does not allow them to have sex. As a consequence of which most of them are phychologically sexually frustrated. That implies that though they may not have any sexual urge in physical terms yet the idea of sex does invade their minds when they see couples in the society. It is quite relevant to pen down the expressions regarding sexual feelings of one of them, who said,

"Eh gal sade dimag which jadon asin aapne pind which hunde han tan nahin aundi. Kyonki ethe tan sab sade bhai-behan ne. Par jadon asin kise dusri jagah jande han tan lokan noon dekhke asi sochde han je asin bhi aadmi-jan aurat hunde taan asi bhi shadi karde te bache jamde. Par eh-gal da saade dimag which aana tan toofan aan wali gal hai. Eh taan oh aag hai jehri jwani which lagdi hai te ant which saadi chita jalan te bujdhi hai (For us sex is not a bodily phenomenon but when we see people around, then the idea of sex enters our mind. We think had we been men or women we would have married. It is a fire which starts burning in the youth and gets extinguished only when our pyre is set on fire)."

The hijras are a sexually frustrated lot and the data lend support to this argument. Out of the 19 cases, as many as 13 (case Nos. 2, 4, 5, 6, 8, 11 and 13 to 19) do express their sexual incapabilities. Then what do they do? Most of them say that they (other hijras and not themselves) act as passive reactors and perform sodomy. It is very interesting to note that none of them tells that he himself ever deviates from the type of life hijras are supposed to live. And as such most of them do not say that they themselves act as homo-sexual or passive reactors. But they blame others for acting in the said way. The point is that no one accepts that he does it but they blame each other for doing the some. In fact, in city like Agra, some of these people act as homosexuals and play as passive reactors. A doctor at Baroda, who treated one hijra for skin disease told the researcher that such diseases are common among them due to the fact that many normal people go to the hijras, pay a small sum of Rs. 2 or Rs. 5 and have sex, especially homosexuality with them. It is. perhaps, due to the feeling to have sex which motivates many hijras to indulge into accessive use of abuses and passing of sexual overtures to others and sometimes to females also. By making overture to other, the author understands that they are able to have some type of oral sexual satisfaction.[20]

The sexual frustration does have its impact on the role performance of hijras. It was revealed by some of them that sometimes they do not feel like going to perform the dance as they feel fed up with their sexual incapabilities. At number of times their awkward sexual utterances create problematic situations and even lead to some type of quarrel with general public. At times, the situation warrants police intervention. This way, their earnings are curtailed. Also they have then problem in operating in that area.

With reference to the discrimination, wrath of hatred and frustration faced by them on many fronts, many may ask a question that what is it which keeps them moving along in the society? This question as such is very significant from the point of view of role performance. The reason being that each and every individual in society revolves around certain motivating factors and which invariably refer to reward structure. The reward structure, if one may say so, is the pivot of role expectations. In the case of hijras, with special reference to the discussion carried under sections on identity crisis and recruitment, the continuity of their role is conditioned by many factors. One such factor is recruitment of new hijras in the Dera which provides continuity to hijra cult and helps in its institutionalization. In the context of continuity of role, it is the socialization first and then the question of survival which compels them to continue. But more then that, to author, it is the rewards which their role can have that hold a predominant place in their thoughts and practical life which provides continuity and make hijras to continue with their role.

There are two type of rewards which help in the perpetuation of hijra role. One is the monetary gains and second is the fame which they can earn by virtue of their talents and good deeds in their own community.

When asked about what are their normally accepted economic rewards, the respondents came out with vivid explanations. The variations in their economic expectations are caused by two things. One, the type of class of the Jajman and two, the standard of the hijra himself. The minimum expected Badhai (reward which they have) is Rs. 11/- or Rs. 21/-. Most of the time, such a meagre amount as reward is asked by the hijras from the people belonging to socio-economically lower class. This is not only the expectation of a less recognised hijra but also of well-known among the hijra community. To quote from one interview with chief of a Dera, who said,

> "Money is our main consideration as without it no one can live in the society. But the happiness of a Jajman is also our major consideration. We know how hard it is to earn. We, therefore, do not trouble poor people. Nowadays the things are so expensive due to rising prices that pressing for a big amount from a poor person is like killing him".

This partly explains their social concern on the one hand and the viability of getting the expected rewards on the other. From the said minimum their range of Badhai goes up alongwith the status of the family to which they go for the performance of dance. They demand Rs. 31/-to Rs. 51/-from those families where the head of the household is working as a clerk or an employee belonging to class three cadre. From a petty businessman or an official of relatively high status they charge Rs. 101/-and a suit or a saree. From people living in big bungalow they charge nothing less than Rs. 251/- or so and a suit or saree of good standard. The author accompanied a group of hijras to a bungalow at Patiala where he saw them, after putting up their dance, demanding a Badhai of Rs. 251/-and a suit or saree of latest fashion. The resident of that banglow offered Rs. 101/-and suit. The hijras refused to accept and continued to insist for Rs. 251/-. When the hijras saw their demand being turned down, the senior hijra took out Rs. 251/-from his pocket and a saree from the bag and offered it to the lady of the house as a Badhai on the birth of a son in that family. This clever act of hijra was certainly an impelling one for the resident as people of the immediate neighbourhood had also come to watch. Finally, the lady of the house had to bow before the demand of the hijra. It is important to note that the hijras do have their clever ways of extracting Badhai. When asked, why do not they agree to accept whatever is offered by the residents, they answer that when one is in a position to pay, it is our right to get that. According to them Rs. 251/-is the minimum which they expect from people living in big bungalows. The rationale for this is that the rich people should give more *daan* to the hijras as they have the resources and income. The hijras insist that it is their right to expect, demand and get that amount of money. Case 15, reacting sharply to author's suggestion that they should not ask for heavy amount but acecpt whatever is offered, remarked,

> "Kyon na paisa lein. Kisi ke marne par hum kisi ke ghar se pani bhi nahin pite. Aise moke pe agar koi lakh rupia bhi de to hum nahin lenge. Hum apna hak sirph do mokon par mangte hain. Ek ladke ke janam par or dusra ladke ki shadi par. Isi liye hamara logon se unki smarthata ke lihaz se mangna koi buri baat nahin. Yeh dono moke to khushi ke moke hote hain. (Why should not we ask for money? We do not even take water at a place where some death has occurred. We will not accept even if we are offered one lakh rupees from that house. We demand money only on two happy occasions, the birth of a male child and marriage of the boy)."

The above description of the monetary expectations which the hijras have from people and the general description of their economic conditions highlighted in the general socio-economic profile point out one very significant dimension of hijras' life, i.e., their economic aspect. In view of this it is not wrong to argue that on an average a hijra has an income of Rs. 1000/-and above a month. Besides money, they do get clothes and other eatables/grocery as a part of their Badhai. All this add to their general economic well-being. At the same time we also know that there are a few among them who lead a life of economic hardship. Let's compare their economic condition with a labourer or a lower class employee and see what is the difference. In the words of hijras only, an employee has to manage a family with his limited means; whereas hijras do not have any family to support or any children to bring up. Therefore, they see their economic condition as better than that of a low paid employee. That is what motivates them to continue in this role. The other reason specified by them for the continuation of this role is that even if they leave this occupation and start up with labourer's job, what will they get out of that? According to them they will not be able to survive. It is, therefore, the income part of their life which continues to motivate them. The importance of and the extent to which the economic aspect influences the hijras can be clear from the case of case 7 who has already been referred to earlier in the context of motive of seeking recruitment. He provides a logical description of how his poor economic conditions on the one hand and good economic conditions of a hijra he knew attracted him to get himself castrated and become hijra.

Case 7, a huge ugly looking hijra comes from a poor scheduled caste family of a town in Punjab. His parents have been working as sweepers. Born as a normal boy he acquired primary education but could not continue in the school due to poverty. Since the economic condition of the family was quite deplorable, he after leaving the school at the age of ten, started helping his parents in their work.

At the age of twenty he got married to a scheduled caste girl, separated himself from his parents and started his independent family life. He came into contact with a local hijra and established relation with them. He was very close to the head hijra of the same town. He used to work as a sweeper but he left that work at the age of about twenty four and started getting his livelihood from that head hijra.

Meanwhile, his wife died, leaving behind two sons. The sons were adopted by his relatives. He started living an independent life and subsequently even started staying with the head hijra in his Dera. His long association with that head hijra, not only brought them very close to each other, but also strengthened latter's faith in the former. In the process, the latter also disclosed about his assets, like gold jewellery, houses, cash and other valuable items. Former's learning about all this had a flabbergasting impact upon him. He said, "I thought I could become very rich by becoming a hijra. In fact, the inheritance of the property of the head hijra could only be possible in my becoming so. Thus, one day I made this offer to my Guru who became very happy."

This way, at the age of thirty two when the head hijra was about to die, he underwent castration operation performed upon him by a doctor. By becoming hijra he, thus, became chela (disciple) and legal heir of the head hijra. The other chelas of the Dera accepted Prem (Case 7) as their Guru. By getting his position legitimised through his acceptance by chelas of the former Guru he got all the property of his Guru and got the authority over two areas in that town.

He did not have any formal training for this profession. Since he inherited the Dera he automatically became the head. After becoming the head, he never went for dancing. When this fellow was working as a mere sweeper he could earn only Rs. 80/- to Rs. 100/- a month, but as a hijara he could get Rs. 80/- to Rs. 100/- and sometimes more a day through his chelas. He clearly expressed that he joined these hijras for money. According to him, he can earn more and live as a rich man. Both the jobs, i.e. that of sweeper and hijra, according to him, are of low category, but he does not mind being a hijra. To him, it is better to earn more and enjoy rather than doing a job which involves more arduous tasks and little returns.

The case 7 clearly indicates that financial considerations have a very vital role to play in their motivation and also for the prepetuation of the role. In fact, like case 7, there are thouands of hijras in big cities who undergo castration operation. Mr. Kharaiti Lal Bhola, President of all India Hijra Kalyan Sabha (All India Hijra Welfare Society) submitted a memorandum to Prime Minister, Rajiv Gandhi for his intervention in the matter relating to secret and illegal castration operations which according to him, are on the increase in the country[19]. It was explicitly stated in the views that such castration are organised by head hijras or Gurus for the purposes of having more chelas to earn money. The economic aspect, therefore, is the most significant factor in making many normal males as hijras.

Besides the said financialattr actions, there is another very significant dimension associated with economic conditions of hijras which is related to their fame, respect and regard within the hijra community. By and large, the financial conditi on of the hijra determines his status in the hijra community. Those, who are relatively rich, have higher status then those who are poor. A more detailed discussion will be carried out in this context in the section dealing with hijra organization, yet from the point of view of the perpetuation of the role, it is desirable to state that the weekness to have higher status and authority in one's community make hijras to continue with their role. Also, it is within their own community that they can have a place and chance to achieve the position of domination therefore, they continue with their role.

To avoid any misconception regarding the relationship between economic condition and position in the community it may be made obvious that the wealth is no doubt an important aspect but at the same time reputation of the hijra in the community and the means through which wealth has been appropriated are also crucial constituent of one's status. Just to cite the case 7 who inherited wealth of Guru and has been able to become head and have few chelas, is not respected within his community. He is in some way an outcaste. But those who have accepted case 7 as their Guru and are working for him do it because of their own motive of getting a territory for practice of hijra cult.

However, in the light of the above description it is not wrong to argue that the continuity of role, in spite of the stresses and strains involved, is the function of economic dismension of hijras in general. Along with that the sense of becoming superior and weakness to acquire authority further create a tendency among hijras to continue with their present role.

NOTES AND REFERENCES

1. Walfred, A. Anderson and Frederick B. Parker, *Society : Its Organization and Operation*, New Delhi, Affiliated East-West Pvt. Ltd., 1966, p. 68.
2. S.L. Sharma, *Development—Socio-Cultural Dimensions*, Jaipur, Rawat Publications, 1986, pp. 17-18, according to Sharma, traditions represent the continuity of social heritage, institutions form the fabric of society, values imply the cherished ideals and solidarities signify the crystallized form of human craving for reaching out to others to form we groups.
3. Anderson, *et al.*, *op. cit.*, 1, p. 68.
4. C.H. Cooley, *Human Nature and Social Order*, New York, Charles Scriloner's Sons, 1902, pp. 1-2, quoted in Anderson, *et al.*, *op. cit.*, 1, p. 68
5. G.H. Mead, *Mind, Self and Society*, Chicago University Press, 1934.
6. Melvin, L. Kohn, "Social Class and Parental Values", *American Journal of Sociology*, Vol. 64, 1959, pp. 337-51.
7. Mead, *op,, cit.*, 5.
8. For details see, Neil J. Smelser and William T. Smelser (eds.) (*Personality and Social Systems* New, York, Willey, 1963.
9. Urie Bronfenbrenner, "Socialization and Social Class", in E.E.

Maccoby, *et. al.* (eds.), *Readings in Social Psychology*, New York Rinehart and Winston, 1958 ; cf. Leonard Brown & Philip Selznick, *Sociology*, New York, Harper and Row Publishers, 1968, p. 100.

10. Broom and Selznick, *Ibid.*

11. Luis, H. Gray, "Eunuchs", in James Hashings (ed.). *Encyclopaedia of Religion and Ethics*, Vol. V, New York, Charles Scribner's Sons, 1908. p. 581.

12. *Ibid.*

13. Dr. G.R. Salunke, of "Cult of the Hijras", *The Illustrated Weekly, of India*, August 8, 1976, p. 14.

14. Peter Worsley, *Introducing Sociology*, Harmondsworth, Penguin Books, 1677, p. 295.

15. Mead, *op. cit.*, 5.

16. S F. Nadel, *The Theory of Social Structure*, Cohen and West Ltd. 1957.

17. Erving Goffman, *Encounters : Two Studies in Sociology of Interaction*, Britain, Penguin Books, 1972.

18. Peter, M. Blau, *The Dynamics of Bureaucracy*. University of Chicago Press, 1963. The author discusses how exchange in role relationships becomes an important and regulating factor.

19. *Tribune, The*, "40,000 Castrated Every Year" (UNI, News Item), 12 Oct. 1986.

4

Hijras : An Organized Existence

The last part of the study concentrated on the analysis of the identity crisis, role-identification, recruitment, socialization, role taking and role performance of hijras. On the basis of which it is desirable to argue that human beings, in order to make their existence social, enter into social alliances with others, from relationships and develop certain patterns of social interaction. Most of the time their interaction is confined to those possessing similar social, economic, psychological and physical attributes. The formation of relationships with each is just not a natural phenomenon but a social signifying interdependence of human beings for the fulfilment of certain needs. Not only that, such formations instil in them a sense of socio-economic and psychological security. That subsequently determines for individuals a sense of being in the world and as units of a specific type of group of individuals. The institutionalization of one's existence and sustenance of one's being in the world becomes possible only through an organized living implying thereby a regulated life and life style.

In terms of the existing sociological writings the organized living provides individuals a social fabric, a metaphor whose implications suggest that human relations are closely interwoven. The appearance of strains in one part of the fabric may weaken the whole set of relationships, thus, reducing a social group to mere individuals unconcerned with each other. The organized living, however, tries to avoid the strains by evolving certain ways and means through which the trouble makers are constrained, punished and isolated. Therefore, it helps in diminishing the possibilities of any disharmony in the society. Since the organized living is 'deliberately constructed and reconstructed for the attainment of certain goals[1] ; by individuals in the society, the major function of any social organization, therefore, can be described as problem solving, *management and resolution of conflict* (emphasis mine), and fostering of cooperation and accommodation within that group[2]. Thus for any human being life without becoming a constituent unit of any social group or organization is very difficult to lead. It becomes more difficult in the case of those who are otherwise rejected by the society. In the context of such individuals, it is observed by many scholars that they form separate sub-culture and try to carry on their activities. In the context of hijras it has also been noted that they being rejected by the society from their own world, a hidden one.

Now the immediate question could be, what after that ? The analysis in the previous chapter brought into view the fact that they seek membership of hijra homes thereby enter into an organized way of living. With regard to their organization it can be stated that in the Indian society, the hijras are living in numerous small organizations which, according to a recent news published in a daily newspaper, number 450. These organizations are further divided into 1,500 subdivisions and 35,000 small offices[3]. The said organizations are nomenclatured as Akhada, Dera, Sthan and Gaddies. Besides they also like in small groups and each group in itself constitutes an independent organization. By and large, the location of their homes is found on the fringe of the cities and towns throughout India. The larger Akhadas are located in large towns, such as Ahmedabad, Baroda, Petlad, Rajkot, Jamnagar, Bombay Panipat, Patiala, Ludhiana,. Jalandhar and many other towns[4]. There are Gaddies existing in Delhi, Gwalior, Jhansi, Bhopal Lucknow, Jaipur, Kanpur and Agra. Though these people do not have any organization at international level yet according to some observations, they have regional confederations which meet for joint celebrations[5].

The organized existence of hijras is indicated of the fact that like any other social organization they do have an institutionalized code of conduct, a value system, specific style of living, and the like. Assuming that like deviant groups the hijras have developed a sub-culture of their own and have organizational set-up for their own welfare it is expected that they, with the help of their organization, put up some defence against any societal sanction to reject their behaviour. In fact, as Becker[6] would put it, "members of all deviant groups of course have one thing in common, i.e. their deviance. It gives them a sense of common fate of being in the same boat. From a sense of common, from having to face same problems, they develop a deviant sub-culture ; a set of perspectives and understanding about that the world is like and how to deal with it and a set of routine activities based on those perspectives". Following Becker's statement, can it be expected that the hijras like the underworld organizations, also develop a perspective through which they are able to defend themselves. The specific questions in this context could be ; what is the nature of hijra organization ? What type of rules and regulations are developed ? Do the functions of hijra organization help in development of anti-society gestures and behaviour ? Are the rules of hijra organization are anti-society ?

The above stated large number of organizations of hijras existing throughout India are independent, autonomous units. At the same time each of these units is related with other units either due to regional affilations or other organizational links. Each Gaddi or Dera is headed by a leader known as Guru and has other occupant known as chelas, who normally number 5 to 10. The living arrangement of Hijra Dera is parallel to family organization. The head of the household is the Guru, regarded as mother, and all the chelas are considered as sons and daughters. Though all the chelas, as per the role requirements are supposed to act as females and make a, as Nanda argues, third gender role, yet gender distinctions are maintained within the Dera. A hijra, either male[7] or female[8] who performs dancing is recognized as daughter whereas the drum beater and harmonium player is called as son. Notwithstanding the gender distinctions drawn on the basis of role performed the important dimension of hijra Dera is that it has a patterned set of role relationships.

At the top of the hierarchy is the Guru, who has full authority and control over his chelas. On the other hand, the chelas occupy varying positions in accordance with their experience and talents within the Dera. The relationships though remain asymmetrical throughout their life yet are governed by the norm of reciprocity. There are certain norms which also regulate the behaviour of Guru towards chela and that of chela towards Guru. These norms in a way, as shall be obvious from the ensuing discussion, are rules exhibited in terms of rights and duties of the various inhabitants of Hijra Dera.

Since the Guru is placed at the highest ebb of the hierarchy, as has also been noted earlier in the context of socialization, he has every right to exercise his authority to restrict and control the behaviour of his chelas. No chela can challenge the authority of his Guru and also cannot dare to put his order at defence. The non-conformists to Guru's authority are seriously dealt with. The Guru makes use of his legitimate right of exercising his authority and punishing the culprits. No objection is raised against the will of Guru and no resistance is put against his authority as such. According to a respondent, "Guru di izzat Rab nalon wadh ke karidi hai, chahe o' sanu mare, chahe kutte, jo saza bhi deve, asi usnoo mande haan" (We respect our Guru more than God. He may beat us or whatever punishment he gives, we undergo that). It has also been found that a Guru can sell and buy his chelas. Once a chela is sold out, his relations with the old Guru change. Though the former may continue to respect his Guru, but the authority of the Guru over his chela thereafter changes. The relationship becomes very formal as the new Guru gets authority over him. Then a chela cannot go to any other Dera. He remains under the direct command of new Guru. His mobility is restricted and as such cannot get chelaship anywhere. The incidence of buying and selling is not very popular among hijras. The chelas, in general, work with the Guru, with whom they have sought recruitment. Whatever they earn throughout the day, they give that to their master. The Guru takes his share and distributes the rest among all the chelas. There is no specified way for distributing the earnings, but it is found that Guru keeps the larger share with him. This is due to the fact that Guru is the head of the Dera and has to keep some money for unforeseen days and off seasons.

Contrary to all this, a chela has no authority and autonomy. He has to fully depend upon the Guru for the fulfilment of his demands. The concept of rights and duties of both will be clear when we take a glance at the role obligations of Guru and chela towards each other. Let us see them separately.

The first function, which a Guru has to perform, as has already been stated, is to make recruitment and socialization which possibly has many implications for hijra organization and hijra cult.

The interviews held with hijras revealed that theiror ganizations performed multiple functions having great influence upon the perpetuation of hijra cult. The first function, therefore, refers to recruitment and socialization of new members. Though a great deal regarding the said function has already been discussed in details yet this aspect of their organization does need to be mentioned here as this is the major function providing continuity to the cult. In the context of recruitment and socialization the respondents were asked the question, why do they recruit new members when some of them hate the present life and are dissatisfied to a great extent. According to the respondents, since they are biologically negativating reproduction, they do wish to have someone to look after them in times of distress and old age. The Gurus who initiate recruitment and socialize the inmates claim that "the young recruits are our sons and daughters and they are the ones who are going to look after us when we get old. After all the body does not continue to function. If they are not there then we have a very tough time ahead. Think of those hijras who do not have anyone to care for them in the old age, they are suffering and have plenty of problems." One of them made a remark in local (Punjabi) dialect "Jeevan di Gaddi vi patri ton leh jayegi te murke enna putan-dhiyan de karan te hi patri te aani hai (The train of life will be off the rails any time and it will be put back on the rails only by these sons and daughters)." The major reason for recruitment and socialization, therefore, is to secure the future, both socially and economically.

It was noted that recruitment is, by and large, voluntary but at the same time there are occasions when the coercive methods are also used. Leaving aside the way recruitments take place the enquiries regarding how the organizations carry on the recruitments revealed that whenever they (hijras) go to anybody's place where the male child has taken birth, one of the function of taking the child into one's lap is to determine and check the sex of the child. The claim of the hijras is that they take away any child born with defective genitals. According to them it is their customary right. Elaborating on the basic rationale of getting such a child, the hijras in general say that if they do not take away such children then how shall they be able to maintain the continuity of their cult. The author's scepticism about such a practice and custom increased on his enquiry from some of the leading hospitals of the country regarding there being any incidence of any child born as such during the last one decade since there was not even a single case where a child was born with defective genitalia. But the hijras insist upon this and do cite examples. Some of them even told during their interview that their detection at late age led to their recruitment and in some cases against the resistance of their parents.

This claim of the hijras is strengthened by the general belief about them prevailing in the Indian society. According to Nanda[9]—

> "Indian belief and the hijras' own claims commonly attribute the impotence of hijra as a male to a hermaphrodite morphology and physiology...implying hermaphroditism as standard reason given for joining the community—and also for recruiting them (emphasis mine)."

Whatever may be the contesting claims of the heads of Hijra Homes the fact remains that recruitments are made by Gurus through various means. Therefore, the possibility of recruiting children with defective genitalia is not exceptional but an acceptable proposition. From the point of view of providing continuity to their organization, which is the most significant and crucial function of the Gurus, the Gurus are always on the look out for an opportunity to bring in the new recruits.

The recruitment, however, is not an end of the responsibility of the hijra organization and the Guru. Beyond that there is a most difficult task for the Gurus and hijra organization, i.e., the socialization and training of the hijras. Their belief is that until and unless the iron is put in the fire and moulded accordingly no shape can develop. To them, a new recruit in the Hijra Dera is like raw iron and which, according to them, can be given any shape by moulding it. Similarly, socialization of new recruit is the one function which is performed by the hijra organization and Guru, in particular.

The socialization and training, as was noted in the earlier chapter, have manifold functions for the hijras. First, in preparing them for the discharging of their professional duties. Second, the Guru has to have some kind of exchange with others in the community. Basically, these general norms pertain to the customs which they have to observe.

Here is the description of some of the popular customs prervailing in the hijra community which all the members are supposed to observe. First, whenever, a hijra guest comes to pay a visit to a hijra Dera the host hijra and others in the Dera will give him respect and honour by serving him to the best of their capacities. When the guest goes back to his place, at the time of departure, the host will pay a certain amount to the guest as 'Shagun'. This amount varies according to the status of the guest. Generally, this is Rs. 11/-, Rs. 21/- and may even go to the extent of Rs. 101/-.

Second is the custom of accepting the young hijra as daughter-in-law or bride by the head of the Dera when the former steps into the profession and starts earning his livelihood. Widely known as initiation ceremony, this occasion is called as red letter day in the life of a hijra. He/she vows to perform his/her role obligations with full honesty and for the happiness of the Guru. On that day, the Guru invites his nears and dears to witness the ceremony. The Guru holds a feast and the guests are honoured with Shagun and new clothes as gifts. That day the guests also offer Shagun to the Guru, like it is done on any wedding in a Hindu society. Sometimes, apart from accepting the new comer as a daughter-in-law, the Guru accepts his chela as his bride and celebrates Suhagraat. In this affair there is no bridegroom and no sexual act as such is performed. This is merely a ritual.

Another custom is of holding small feast on a city or regional level. This is mostly done to have a get-together, joint celebrations followed by a meeting to discuss their problems. In general terminology such meetings are known as Panchayat. Basically, the entire socialization process organized and carried out by the hijra organization lays emphasis upon the integration and solidarity of the hijra community.

Secondly, Guru being regarded as the mother of her chelas, it is, therefore, her primary duty to administer the household affairs and look after the general welfare of her chelas. How does the Guru do so ? This is basically done by gratifying the needs of the chelas. The needs of the hijras are not alike and, therefore, differ from individual to individual and Dera to Dera. However, there are certain common needs such as good food, clothes, accommodation and pocket allowance. The gratification of the said needs is very essential for the maintenance of harmony within the Dera and avoidance of any sort of disregard and disrespect from other Deras with which the Dera under question has any link. The reason being that one often comes across hijras making certain remarks against other Deras wherever they think that the members are not looked after well. In view of the possibility of earning any disrespect, the Gurus try their best to meet the needs of their chelas.

Besides the day-to-day requirements, there are, at times, certain specific type of demands made by the chelas which the Gurus allow with certain reservations. For example, the demand on the part of a member to visit other Dera to meet his friends. The Gurus always have fear of losing an inmate if he mixes up too much with the hijras of another Dera. According to hijras such suspicions are, to a very great extent, true because there have been cases of chelas who, under the influence of others, have left their respective Deras and, thus, jeopardised relationships among local hijras. The other demand made by some of them is in terms of permission to meet their parents. Such a demand comes from very few cases. For instance, case 4 was found to be maintaining relationship with her family. She goes to her mother and sometimes her mother comes to her. Such meetings, according to hijras, are very painful and emotion evoking. Because the parents continue to suffer the stigma of their child's asexuality. The respondent, who is a Guru, told that whenever the mother of case 4 comes to her child the people in the street call her as "khusre di Maa" (mother of hijra). Such a behaviour on the part of others irritates the mother and at times there have been quarrels also. Since the Dera gets into trouble because of the visit of any relation of any inmate, very often such meetings are restricted. But the other reason as hijras put it, is that in certain cases some hijras who used to meet their parents very often were caught passing on to them money and jewellery of the Dera. In view of the possibility of occurrence of any such problem the requests for frequent meetings are very often turned down. As such only limited meetings are allowed and that too the hijra is asked to go and visit her parents.

The third most important function of the Guru is to maintain link between the members of his Dera and that of the other Dera. It is a significant feature of the Hijra Deras that their members approach each other at the time of distress and mis-happenings. All these obligations on the part of the Guru when fully discharged by him, help the hijras in their integration with their total community.

On the other hand a chela has the following role obligations to perform. Firstly, to serve the Guru who has brought him up and made him capable of earning. At the same time chelas have to respect and honour the elders of the community. Secondly, it is only with the permission of the Guru that a chela can move out, i.e. without former's permission a chela cannot go to see his parents(if living) or anywhere else he wishes to go.

Besides the role obligations which the occupants of different statuses have to discharge, the hijra community is a fully stratified society on the basis of authority. Like society, in general, hijras do observe differences among themselves on the basis of sex, caste, income and wealth. This type of differentiation forms the basis of stratification among them. There is guru and chela relationships indicating one as higher and the other as lower in status. Male hijra is more dominant than female hijra in decision-making within the hijra communtiy. A hijra with more income is recognised as a person of high status, whereas a poor one is considered a person of low status. No consideration is given to religion but caste considerations are sometimes present. Hijras belonging to low caste, like jamadars (Chuhra) etc. are not allowed to enter the kitchen. They are devoid of certain privileges while others are not. For example, the movement of those belonging to lower caste is restricted within the house permises. They cannot touch the utensils in which the head of the household eat. They are asked to sleep away form the other hijras. Therefore, one finds practice of some kind of untouchability among hijras. But at the same time it is important to mention that all Hijra Deras do not follow this type of practice of untouchability.

In spite of the fact that there is differentiation and stratification among them, the hijras continue with their distinct culture and life. There is one significant force which has a vital role in this context. This force is the Hijra Panchayat. A number of questions arise as : what is the 'Panchayat' ? When is it held ? What is the structure of Panchayat ? How the election of Panchayat held is made and how other senior members are elected ? What are the function of the Panchayat ? The Hijra Panchayat can be simply described as the assembly of hijras from all over the country or those belonging to a particular state or a city. The place, month, day and time of such an assembly is predecided and no formal invitation is sent to any of the members. Since the hijras have prior information all are obliged to attend the Panchayat. Mostly, such a Panchayat is held on the occasion of some festival like Diwali, Dussehra, Baisakhi, etc. Another occasion on which these people meet is at the death of hijra and also for the celebration of the anniversary of the dead. This is perhaps the most important occasion in the community. On this occasion a feast is organized by a chela to pay tributes to his dead Guru. In Punjab this feast is known as 'Guru di Roti'. The food served is Pacca food prepared in pure ghee. It lasts for seven-eight days. For example, every year, such feast is held at many places at the instance of some chelas. in order to pay tribute to their dead gurus. Joint feast is also organized by a few Deras on the occasion of Baiskhi in Punjab. These are the main occasion when the hijra community gets together.

During such gatherings, which are called Panchayats, two-three or sometimes five-six heads are elected. The criteria for election are very simple. Only the well known elders, who are experienced and enjoy good reputation, are elected as heads and they thereby get authority over the whole assembly. Alongwith the heads, few others who are local, are given a place in the Panchayat as members of the Panchayat.

Besides the regional or national Panchayats there are local hijra Panchayats headed by the heads of the local Deras. The head of Dera is always the eldest member having overall authority over his chelas or companions. After the death of Guru, the eldest chela in the Dera takes charge of the Dera. There is the norm of inheritance of authority. It is always the eldest who inherits the command. The main functions which the hijra Panchayat performs are the following :

The main function of the Panchayat is to get together after an interval of a few months (months are not specified). The basic purpose of this is to look into the problem of hijras and to find out their possible solutions. One problem which invariably comes up, is the wooing of chelas of one Dera by the head of other Dera. The hijra organization solves such problems either by restoring back the chela or getting some compensation to the loser. Both type of solutions are acceptable to the hijra community. Also such solutions put an end to the problem. The other problem occurring very often pertains to violation of territorial jurisdiction. For instance, if any Guru or chela is facing some territorial adjustment problem, it is the duty of Panchayat to find out the best possible solution which can be acceptable to the total community.

The second function, which the Panchayat performs, is the distribution of the territories. Each Dera of hijras has a definite jurisdiction, i.e., a number of villages and towns where its members can operate for the performance of their role. Violation of territory is strictly prohibited. Anyone who violates the territorial jurisdiction is punished by the Panchayat. The punishment can be in terms of fine or ex-communications from the community.

When such Panchayats are held, certain sets of norms are formulated by the heads of the Panchayat. These norms are supposed to be observed by all the members. Non-observers or those showing disobediency to those norms are liable to punishment. This is the third function which falls within the purview of Panchayat. To do justice, give punishment to the law breakers and to reward those who do well for the community are described as the biggest functions of the Panchayat.

Another occasion on which hijras of nearby towns come together is the time when any hijra dies. As per the rules of hijra organization no relation of the decased is permitted to attend the funeral. Probably no one has ever seen the funeral of a hijra except for hijras themselves. The death of hijra is not taken lightly by the community. All the rituals and ceremonies are performed so that the dead does not have rebirth as hijra. There are two points of view regarding the death rituals among the hijras. One point of view comes from the hijras belonging to north India and another from the hijras belonging to South. Those, who belong to Northern India, put forth the description of their death rituals which is similar to the death rituals observed by people belonging to different religions. Accordingly, the last rites of a hijra are performed according to the religion to which he belongs. A Hindu will, therefore, be cremated and a Muslim will be buried. Since no relative of the deceased is allowed to attend the funeral at the time of death, it is, therefore, the duty of the hijra community to dispose of the dead. Non-attendance by any near relation and the claim of the hijras that they alone are permitted to perform the last rites, however, is not explicit in the sense that whether this is a strictly regulated phenomenon or just a claim. But one explanation which seems quite plausible here is that it is perhaps due to property reasons that hijras do not allow the real relations to attend funerals. If a hijra dies at the age of eighty and above. his pyre is taken out at midnight with musicians playing music.

Hijras, who belong to South India and particularly to Madras region, tell about a different type of death ritual. According to them the dead is buried in his own home. If the home does not belong to the dead, then the dead is taken out of the home at mid-night when no one is there to watch. The dead is taken out in the standing position by three-four of his companions. They take the dead to the jungle and dig a deep ditch. They put two three quintals of salt into the ditch and bury the dead in a standing position. While taking to the jungle he is given beatings. After burying the dead they offer a prayer to the goddess to give salvation to the dead.

The hijra organization, in particular, owe their origin to Goddess Bahuchara. The temple of the goddess is situated in Gujarat near Ahmedabad. Though the Bahuchara Mata is their main goddess yet the hijras of north India do worship the local and regional goddesses, like Vaishnu Devi, Mansa Devi, etc. But there are hardly any mythological justifications revealed by the hijras. However, in the case of Bahuchara Mata there are a large number of stories. Salunke [10] argues, "the Bahuchara worship in the form of the vulva is related to the ritual of castration. The idea is to identify one-self with the deity which is done by donning feminine dress". Since it gives them a sense of identity, so violation of it is considered threat to hijra cult. According to Salunke, violation of any such rule is punishable by the hijra community's court of law, i.e., hijra Panchayat[11]. It is, therefore, within the purview of hijra community to provide religious symbols.

Last but not the least, the hijra organization at the level of the total community and hijras at the level of their own Dera have a very important function relating to the relationship between the hijras and the society at large. Though much has been said on socialization, training and other things which make a hijra a well- behaved member of the community yet the hijra organization also takes specific care to maintain good relationships between them and the society. During the hijra Panchayat it is, time and again, emphasized by their, leadership that they should maintain cordial relationship with their jajmans. There is no denying the fact that the people in the society have a derogatory attitude towards the hijras. Even great epic, like Mahabharata indicates them as lowest. The following phrase makes it very explicit. "Malechhas are the dirt of humanity, oilmen are the dirt of Malechhas, Hijras are the dirt of oilmen". They are stoned, abused and looked down upon by all and sundry. Notwithstanding, what type of attitude people have towards them the hijra community does not allow its members to get provoked and, tnus, land into some kind of dispute. If ever such a thing happens, the hijra Panchayat takes a judicious view of the matter and punishes its member with suitable fine or any other type of penalty.

Society may hate them, but they respect and bear all the tortures from the society. They lead a secluded life of their own and live in isolation, i.e., away from society. No one goes to them, they meet people only for a short period. After dancing and congratulating the jajman, they take their share and go back to their own places. They never pose any threat to society but always lead a threatened life on account of the derogatory attitude of the people towards them.

NOTES AND REFERENCES

1. T. Parson, *Structure and Process in Modern Societies*, Glanco III, The Free Press, 1960.

2. L. Broom and P. Selzuick, *A Test with Adapted Readings*, Harper and Row, Publishers, Inc., New York, 1973, p. 19.

3. *The Tribune*, 12 October 1986.

4. A.M. Shah, "A Note on Hijadas of Gujarat", *American Anthropologist*, Vol. 63, No. 6, 1961, p. 1328.

5. Thomas, Smith, *Eunuch* : *Modern and Ancient History and Politica Journal*, 1958.

6. Howard, S. Becker, *Outsiders*, London, Free Press, Collier-Macmillan Ltd., 1963, p. 38.

7. A male hijra has a short, flaccid penis. The testicles are not visible.

8. A female hijra has a urinary canal but no vagina.

9. Serena Nanda, "The Hijras of India : Cultural and Individual Dimensions of an Institutionalized Third Gender Role", *J. Homosexuality*, Vol. II (3-4)' 1985, p.38.

5

Summary and Discussion

After having carried out the detailed analyses of various aspects of the life of hijras in India the author arrives at certain definite points. First, a hijra, due to sexual deformity (born as such or castrated later) is a stigmatized person. The stigma of asexuality makes him some kind of an outsider in the society. Second, the stigma not only makes him an outsider in relation to members of the society as such but also isolates him from his family and from the society at large. He, therefore, does not find a space in the family and consequently forced to look for an alternate arrangement for his living. Such a state of isolation from his kith and kins is a compulsion and not a choice. It is so as most of them, as has been noted in the foregoing discussion, express their emotional attachment with their families by saying that they wish to be with their parents, brothers and sisters. But, since their presence in the family attaches a stigma...they have no alternative other than to leave home and live with others of their kind. This leads to the third point that it becomes almost impossible for a hijra to pass either as a male or a female in the society. The identity crises, therefore, force him to accept an alternative way of living in a mini society of hijras. Fourth, the existence of a mini society suggests that there also exists an institutionalized role (the role of a hijra) with well defined mechanism of recruitment, socialization and social control. In the context of institutionalization of a non-normal role, it has been observed that learning of a role, internalization of values of the group and integrity of the group depends upon the said mechanism. The hijra organisation also maintains a strict code of conduct for the regulation of its behaviour of members. Fifth , being a mini society, the cult of hijras represents a sub-cultural system in itself. This system is viewed by the larger society as outside it. Though hijras are conceived to be living as a sub-cultural group, which differs from the society in many ways, yet the hijras maintain tangential contacts with the society at large, i.e., some degree of interaction between them and the society does take place.

Some of the aforementioned characteristic features of hijras, when compared with the characteristics of deviant behaviour, seem to be quite similar and close to each other. In view of which can it be taken for granted that a hijra and his role is deviant? This question needs to be analysed in the light of various theoretical explanations elaborated earlier (introductory chapter) in the context of deviant role.

To begin with the concept of deviant behaviour connotes that it is that action of human being which is anti-normative and essentially goes against the welfare of members of the society. Being harmful it becomes an object of social concern. This precisely that there another dimension, i.e., the public recognition of the act. If public recognition is not there then it is difficult to categorise a behaviour as deviant. In view of this connotation of deviant role, the role of a hijra does not have the property of harm in relation to other members of the society. Also, as witnessed from the analyses the role of hijras is not anti-society. Rather, right from ancient times onward, they have been playing significant roles in the society. In spite of the fact that they were exploited, still in functional terms they served the kings, the princesses and royal women with utmost responsibility and loyalty. Even in the contemporary Indian society they perform two very significant functions. One, by visiting peoples' homes on festive occasions they congratulate and bestow blessings on people and also take away the stigma from any family by taking away any individual with asexuality.

At this juncture two questions come up for consideration. First, if the hijras and their role is not anti-social then, why are they considered outsiders, stigmatized and unfit to live within the family of their origin ? Second, why are they accepted on certain festive occasions ? To begin with the second question first, it is understandable that hijras are accepted because of their functional utility. Basically, it pertains to hijras' claim to take away any hermaphrodite child and, thus, taking away the source of stigma. At this point it is also essential to argue that the acceptance of hijras at festive occasions is also governed by the cultural traditions and beliefs of people in terms of giving alms. Also by and large, people view them with fear of curse and hope of blessing. The basic contradiction in human behaviour which comes into limelight from the analysis of hijras' life is that the people follow pragmatic approach in accepting and rejecting the same thing at two different points of time. More precisely, the human beings accept anything functional to them and reject anything non-functional[1].

In the context of the first question, again the cultural expectations of the society seem to be significantly decisive. The Indian society, in particular, value the individual capacities to procreate. Any individual not capable of reproduction is, therefore, conceived as abnormal. Especially, in the context of such men terms like *Namard* (signifying impotency) is used. Even such persons are called as Hijras. If this being the case then it is understandable that human beings with deformed genitals are stigmatized and singled out in the society. At the same time, it being a biological condition, is also an inevitable phenomenon. It can occur in any family and with any individual. Also the people who get themselves castrated and join the bands of hijras become biologically incapable of reproduction. From the said arguments it can be hypothetically argued that the acceptance and rejection of hijras can also be understood with reference to the cultural expectations of the Indian society.

In terms of the existing conception of deviant behaviour the hijras are not deviant but designated as such due to certain attributes which, in the given cultural gestalt, render them different from others in the society. If this is so then can the existing theoretical formulations on deviant behaviour explain the case of hijras and the role they perform ? Emile Durkheim will regard such a role, though unusual, as an integral aspect of human society and normal. Furthermore, to him, society itself creates deviance as the latter has certain positive functions to perform[2]. Accordingly, the hijras' role can be considered the creation of the society for the performance of certain functions. Durkheim's viewpoint, however, cannot be completely applicable to the case of hijras. The hijras, in no way, offend the collective sentiments which are central to Durkheim. They rather preserve the sanctity of the legal norms by not breaking them. The act of self-emasculation also does not harm the society except for the individual who, by doing so, becomes stigmatized. Even in the context of self-emasculation one has to analyse the conditions which compel individuals to undergo such an operation. One of the cases referred to in the foregoing discussion on hijras reveals that his act of castration was motivated by the economic considerations rather than something inherent in him.

The explanation of a case signifying money as the motivating factor brings the case of hijras very close to Merton's[3] view of structural inequalities and the possible way of achieving certain goals. Here again, as far as the case of castrated hijras is concerned, one can understand that they being in structurally low positions try to earn more by becoming hijras. But Merton's explanation does not have any adequate answer to the case of hijras who are born as hermaphrodites. Therefore, the theory of structural inequalities has significant reference to certain specific category of hijras and, therefore, cannot be applied to the case of born hijras.

The above discussed explanations lack complete application to hijras and thereby fall short of understanding them. The findings suggest that the most important thing in the case of hijras is the stigma from which they suffer and which take them away from their families. At the same time, hijras in the Indian society exist with an institutionalized arrangement which incorporates such individuals in the society. This situation pertains to an atypical type which seeks an explanation for the understanding of hijras in a more meaningful manner. A question, therefore, remains, is there any extant sociological theory which can explain the case of hijras with special reference to the stigma suffered by them. In this context it will be appropriate to take into consideration the theoretical explanations put forth by Goffman, Becker, Parsons and others.

I turn to Goffman[4] because he had examined the phenomenon of stigma and I have found that the hijras are stigmatized. The hijras have a physical deformity which places them at a terrible disadvantage in the society. Following Goffman, one can say that the hijras are something that is "not quite human". The society has developed a belief system which explains his inferiority, and accounts for the dangers presented by a stigmatized person. But the similarity seems to end here. Unlike what Goffman postulates, the hijras do not think of themselves as superior to normal human beings. They have the same self image as the one that the society has of them (cf. case number 2. "A dog's life is better than that of a hijra"). A hermaphrodite might try to pass as either a normal male or female as indicated by Goffman. However, passing as such is not quite successful. On the contrary, once the role of hijra is adopted, the emphasis is on exhibiting the deformity rather than on hiding it. On many occasions when a hijra is dancing on the streets, he will expose himself. It is for this reason that one finds that Goffman's formulations of stigma do not adequately cover the case of the hijras.

Yet, another theoretical formulation that one may consider, is Becker's work on the 'Outsider'. It has been seen above that the hijras are forced to live outside the normal pale of the society and Becker[5] suggests that deviance is a creation of society. A society creates rules whose infraction constitutes deviance. The application of rules to certain groups and the labelling of these groups as outsiders constitutes deviance. Becker further suggests that the outsiders live in a world of their own, creating an institutionalized system with strong historical, legal and psychological justifications for their deviant activity. When one moves into a deviant group one quickly learns to carry on one's activity with a minimum of trouble. He, however, maintains that the belief systems justifying their deviant activity are contraposed to those of the society and the former are deemed to be "right" and the latter "wrong".

Becker's formulation covers a number of the mode of living of the hijras as far as their being outsiders is concerned. There is one crucial aspect which it is not able to explain. The belief system of the hijras does not appear to be contradicting that of the society. They do not seem to have developed justifications which challenge the rules of the society. On the contrary, they respect the normative order of the society and do not pose a threat to it, as long as they remain away from it. The institutionalization on the part of hijras is functional for the society rather than being a threat to it.

Given the partial applicability of Goffman's and Becker's models of 'stigma' and 'outsider', respectively, the Parsonian[6] concept of 'secondary institution' may be considered for giving an explanation of the role of hijras. The secondary institutions emerge in the society in the processes of interaction. Two characteristics are pertinent. First, a secondary institution is not "normal"—it is an organisation of deviants whose existence is not tolerated in the society. Secondly, these are insulated. There is a minimum or only a tangential contact between a secondary institution and the larger society. Prostitution is a typical case for Parsons. In the case of hijras, as we have seen, they team up and live in a highly structured organisation of their own with a code of conduct for the regulation of the behaviour of the fellow members. As far as teaming up and living in an institutional way is concerned, the concept of secondary institution may be applied to the hijra Deras. They are also insulated from the mainstream of social life. But there lies a fundamental difference between the very constitutions and constituents of hijra organisation.

For Parsons it is when deviants are present in sufficiently large numbers in a society and when the mechanisms of social control have failed to restore status-quo-ante that secondary institutions come into operation. The institution of hijras comes very close. structure-functionally, to Parsons' secondary institution. There is, however, a crucial difference between the two which negates his comparability. According to Parsons, when some members of the society find that their needs cannot be gratified by adhering to the norms of the society, they reject these norms and evolve their own. In other words, the onus of deviating falls on the hijras, the situation is just the opposite of what Parsons had visualised. The hijras initially want to conform to the dominant gender-specific norms of the society which does not want them to conform. This contention can be borne out by two sets of data. When we examine the cases in which the hijras voluntarily joined the group, he was carrying out the roles of appropriate to his age and gender within the family as well as without but on discovery of the sexual deformity was hounded out. During The discussion with them, they expressed a strong desire to lead a "normal" life. They longed for the company of their families and wanted to take up jobs. The attempts on the part of some of the cases to run away from the Dera and to pass as normal males or females supported the contention that it is not they who have rejected the society. Thus, the onus of deviating is not on the deviant but on the society.

Having noted the inapplicability of western sociological theory to the paradoxical position of the hijras in Indian society, I would like to mention further a fact that the role of hijra has become extinct in the West. A hermaphrodite is a biological phenomenon and it must be as surely occurring in the West as it does in India. And yet intriguingly enough, there is no sociological role corresponding to it. In the absence of data and, therefore, relying upon the information provided by western scholars in my personal discussions with them about his problem, I can say that such persons are forced to pass either as males or as females. This may be facilitated by modern surgical and medical techniques of comparatively recent origins. However, the role disappeared long before these techniques were perfected and practised.

It is, therefore, the contention of the author that institutionalization of social items is not random but is governed by the modes of cognization. A social institution or a role is not merely a part of a formal social arrangement to be described in structural or functional terms alone. If these have to be made sense of, they must be seen in the context of the cultural gestalt. This is the position that Weber advocates. While one may agree with Weber[7], one should like to go beyond the cognization that will give a clue to the cultural as well as the social systemic formation. In other words, it is how one looks at the world that would affect not only what one will pay attention to, but also how one would organize these.

The specific question that I would like to pose here is the following. Is it possible that there are fundamental differences in the modes of cognization of the West and of India which would plausibly explain the absence of the role in the West and its presence in India ? The modern Western thought works through unmediated dualism of double monism, i.e., works through opposite : fact/value, nature/culture, subject/object, etc.[8]. In terms of this mode of thinking, the universe, inclusive of the socio-cultural domain, is neatly divided into predetermined categories. Anything which does not fall into a niche is defined as an aberration, a deviant case. Any social structure or culture that does not fall into this pattern is immediately labelled as backward, underdeveloped and irrational. It is implicit in this formulation that there is only one type of rationality the means end rationality prevalent in Western societies.

It may, however, be argued that the universe can be made sense of in more ways than one. The Western means end rational world-view is only one of them and, perhaps, not as is claimed. But this is neither the place nor the occasion to offer a critique of Western rational mode of thinking. The point here is that specific socio-cultural items make sense, i.e., can be shown to be rational, only if these are placed in the totality. Taken in isolation they might appear to be irrational, bizarre, deviant, aberrant, etc. This is particularly true if one is working with other cultures.

The role of the hijra may, prima facie, appear to be an aberration in a society which meticulously lays down the "do's" and "don'ts" for males and females. In fact, Hindu society is notorious for its rigidity and narrow scope of the norms. The appearance, therefore, of such a role as that of the hijra poses problems to students of Indian society. The answer cannot be found in an analysis of structure. It has to be sought, as has been mentioned earlier, in the mode of cognization.

The Hindu mode of cognization, is holistic, adaptive and encompassing. The underlying assumption of a unitary universe provides modes of incorporating and, thus, making sense of the apparently paradoxical. The history of Hindu civilization clearly shows, how over millennia, it has incorporated strands from diverse cultures and yet maintained a distinct identity of its own. It is for this reason that the Indian psychiatrist Kakar[9] maintains that Hindu thought allows for the co-existence and unification of what, according to Western thought, may be deemed to be paradoxical.

The author does not follow the attributes that Kakar's formulation ascribes to the hijras. However, the fact remains that despite the negative evaluation of this group by the society, it finds an institutionalized role for itself in the socio-religious life. The hijras are stigmatized as inauspicious and yet on the two most auspicious occasions in the life-cycle, i.e., on births and on weddings, they form an integral part of the celebrations.

Some may argue that the formulation above is incorrect since Hindu thought is almost obsessively concerned with the oppositions of pure and impure[10]. Whereas it is true that Hindu cognitive structures are built up around the opposition of the pure and the impure, a study by Veena Das[11] has shown how this opposition is mediated or ended. In an examination of ritual procedure based upon the Grihya Sutra of Gobhila she has indicated the processes of mediations of oppositions.

Thus, the opposition of male/female gender role does not remain a dualism but is mediated by the role of the hijra. It will not be appropriate to recount an episode from the Mahabharat concerning Arjuna. In the Hindu mythology the Arjun-Krishna pair has been idealised as that of Nara-Narayana. Arjuna has been idealised as the perfect male and Krishna as the perfect incarnation of Vishnu. Arjuna, the perfect male, however, according to the terms of the Pandava's pact with the Kauravas, has to adopt the role of a hijra, Brihannala, and teach singing and dancing to Virata's daughter Uttra for a period of one year while the Pandavas had to remain incognite.

NOTES AND REFERENCES

1. Satish K. Sharma, "Eunuchs : Past and Present", *The Eastern Anthropoiogist*, Vol. 37, No. 4, 1984.

2. Emile Durkheim, "The Normal and the Pathological", in Delos H. Kelly (*ed.*), *Deviant Behaviour : Readings in the Sociology of Deviance*, New York, St. Martin's Press, 1979.

3. R.K. Merton, "Social Problems and Sociological Theory", in R.K. Merton and R.A. Nisbet (*eds.*), *Contemporary Social Problems*, New York, Harcourt, Bruce and World, 1961, pp. 697-737.

4. E. Goffman, *Stigma*, Harmondsworth, Penguin Books Ltd., 1964.

5. Howard S. Becker, *Outsiders*, London, Collier Macmillan Ltd., 1963.

6. Talcott Parsons, *The Social System*,, London, Tavistock Publications, 1952.

7. Max Weber, *Economy and Society* (eds., Roth and Wittch), Berkley, University of California Press, 1978.

8. Oberoi, J.P.S., *Science and Culture*, The Oxford University Press, Delhi, 1978.

9. Kakar, Sudhir, *The Inner World : A Psycho-Analytic Study of Childhood and Society in India*, The Oxford University Press, New York, 1981.

10. Dumont, L., *Home Hierarchicus*, Vikas, Delhi, 1960.

11. Das, V., *Structure and Cognition*, Oxford University Press, Delhi, 1977.

Index